FLIGHT

A Pictorial History from
the Wright Brothers to Supersonic

PUBLISHER'S NOTE

You are about to enjoy the most comprehensive visual record of the history of flight ever assembled in one single volume. Edited by an acknowledged authority, it takes you from the very beginnings up to the late 1950's when presumably we all became aware of the subject from personal observation and experience. Here are those rich, formative years before our own age of awareness, displayed pictorially (over 640 photos) and accompanied by a knowledgeable and pertinent commentary so that we might enjoy its reading over and over again. The British editor may have tended to emphasise the European contribution, but since his expertise in the field is unassailable and since the wealth of detail he has provided is as impressive as in any other published document within our memory, we hope you agree that a small bias is more than compensated for by such a massive compendium of information and entertainment.

Other Pictorial Histories in this Series
Each containing 400-650 illustrations:

RAILWAYS
A Pictorial History of the First 150 Years
by C. HAMILTON ELLIS

SHIPS
A Pictorial History from Noah's *Ark*
to the U.S.S. *United States*
by C. HAMILTON ELLIS

MOTORING
A Pictorial History of the First 150 Years
by L. T. C. ROLT

First Published in this Edition, 1974, by
Peebles Press International Inc.,
140 Riverside Drive, New York, N.Y. 10024

Originally Published by Hulton Press Ltd., London, as
A PICTURE HISTORY OF FLIGHT

© John W. R. Taylor

ISBN 0 85690 009 5

Printed and bound in Gt. Britain by
Redwood Burn Ltd., Trowbridge & Esher.

A Lockheed Lodestar flown by Alaska Star Airlines, 1940-44. (*Picture courtesy of Lockheed Aircraft Corporation*)

FLIGHT

A Pictorial History from the
Wright Brothers to Supersonic

by
JOHN W. R. TAYLOR

PEEBLES PRESS
New York: London

Contents

Foreword to this Edition

This book tells one of the most exciting stories in history. It begins in the age of myth and legend, when only gods and supermen could fly. It shows how generations of men and women longed to share the freedom and adventure of flight, trying first to copy the feathered flapping of the birds that wheeled and soared so effortlessly above their heads.

If courage had been sufficient to match the intricacy and strength of a bird's mechanism, the men who leaped off towers and cliffs, waving their wings of feathers and wood, must surely have earned success. But it was not enough, and many of them died.

Frustrated, other would-be fliers learned at last to raise themselves into the air in baskets carried beneath huge gas-bags of hot air and hydrogen. Drifting like bubbles in the wind, with little chance of choosing their path or destination, they were airborne without really flying. The same is true of the vast majority of people who travel by air today.

To fly is to use the air like a bird, to feel its moods and power through the long, delicate wings of a sailplane, to zoom and dive amid towering cloud castles in a lightplane, to build in a small private room a tiny machine of metal or wood and then to hop joyously around the summer skies, seeing familiar sights from unfamiliar angles, feeling the wind on your face and a freedom in your heart.

How different is commercial air travel – the end product of seven decades of progress since the Wright brothers. The traveller is packed with three hundred others in an air-conditioned cylinder, feeding mind and body on films and pre-cooked meals as the wonders of our world pass below, unseen from a 600 m.p.h. flying armchair at 40,000 feet.

The man who wrote "To travel hopefully is a better thing than to arrive" had never travelled by air. Yet it is the supreme human achievement that 500 million people – equivalent to one in eight of the entire population of the Earth – can be carried each year on scheduled airline services; that millions of acres of land can be made more fertile by aircraft, to grow the food demanded by "exploding" populations; and that the mere threat of the aeroplane's striking power may have ended for ever the danger of world war.

Six hundred and fifty illustrations, many of them so rare that they can be found in no other book, were needed to tell the story of how all this was made possible. Yet the key events can be counted on the fingers of one hand.

First, on 17th December 1903, the American brothers Orville and Wilbur Wright proved it possible for men to fly in a powered aeroplane. Six years later a Frenchman, Louis Blériot, crossed the narrow seas from France to England in a frail monoplane of his own design, pointing the way to a form of travel that would overcome all natural and political barriers.

As the 'thirties drew to a close an Englishman named Whittle and a German named von Ohain perfected a new type of power plant that was fitted in the first jet-planes, to open up a whole new concept of speed and, eventually, comfort and safety in flight.

The last natural obstacle to progress fell on 14th October 1947 when another American, Charles Yeager, smashed through the "sound barrier" and pioneered an age in which speeds could be measured in thousands of miles an hour.

Finally, in 1957, came the Russian achievement which brings our story to its climax. A satellite named *Sputnik I* bleeped its way through space as the first man-made object to defy Earth's gravity and enter orbit, blazing a trail for astronauts to follow. That trail has since led to the Moon, while, nearer Earth, the X–15 rocket-plane has flown at 4,534 m.p.h. and the Concorde airliner carries ordinary men and women at supersonic speeds. All of this has happened within the traditional lifetime of a man – three-score years and ten.

J.W.R.T.

Flight was a challenge
that man could not ignore . . .

What a Dream It Was

FLIGHT was a challenge that man could not ignore. He could walk and run like the beasts and swim like the fishes: only the birds moved in an element that defied his physical prowess. Watching the effortless, soaring flight of the gulls, man felt insignificant, a creature living in a two-dimensional world.

His gods could fly, because all things were possible to them. Greek Hermes and Roman Mercury were winged messengers from Olympus. Khensu in Egypt, the war-god Maris in Japan, the Assyrian winged bull Cherubin, all could fly. The Prophet Elijah rode into heaven on a chariot of fire, and even the Holy Bible has its angels with wings of pure white feathers or gold.

Mythology told of humans who tried to fly. Daedalus and Icarus, who escaped imprisonment by Minos, King of Crete, by flying on wings of feather and wax; Bladud, ninth King of Britain and father of Shakespeare's King Lear, who was killed at the time of Elijah; Wayland the Smith in Scandinavia; and others. Their example caused the deaths of countless 'bird-men' who, for hundreds of years, hurled themselves from towers and cliffs with all-too-frail wings strapped to their arms.

Perhaps, even more than the gods and super-men of mythology, it was the birds themselves that defeated man's efforts to fly until a mere half-century ago. The apparent effortlessness of their flight deceived an age that knew nothing of air currents, or the complex structure and tremendously strong muscles that were hidden under the outward simplicity of a bird's wings. Not until Borelli declared uncompromisingly in 1680 that man lacked sufficient strength in the muscles of his arms and legs ever to sustain his own weight in the air was the reason for the bird-men's failure appreciated. Even then, as late as 1742, the 62-year-old Marquis de Bacqueville tried to flap his way over the Seine, from which he was fortunate to escape with nothing worse than a broken leg.

Gradually, would-be airmen came to realise that they would never fly merely by trying to copy the birds. Something altogether new was needed – just as the wheel, which has no parallel in nature, had to be discovered before movement over land could be made easier.

A few scattered ideas were half-lost in the pages of history. Earliest, perhaps, were the claims of the English scientist-monk Roger Bacon (1214–92), whose *Secrets of Art and Nature*, written about 1250 and translated in 1659, contained

Flight of Fancy

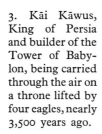

2. Bladud, the British king who tried to fly, came to the throne in 863 B.C. He is said to have killed himself twenty years later when his home-made wings failed and he crashed onto the Temple of Apollo in the city of Trinavantum, which we now call London.

3. Kāi Kāwus, King of Persia and builder of the Tower of Babylon, being carried through the air on a throne lifted by four eagles, nearly 3,500 years ago.

4. This apparatus designed in 1678 by Besnier, a locksmith of Sablé in France, was a variation of the old flapping-wing idea.

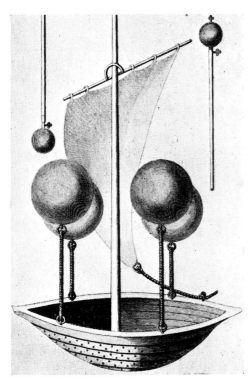

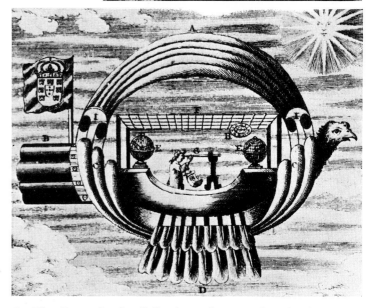

5. De Lana's airship was the first definite design for a lighter-than-air craft. It was intended to be lifted by four thin copper balloons from which all the air had been extracted.

6. The *Passarola*, fancifully drawn by an artist who had never seen it, was really the carriage of a hot-air balloon designed by Gusmão, chaplain to the King of Portugal, in 1709.

the statement that 'It's possible to make Engines for flying, a man sitting in the midst thereof, by turning onely about an Instrument, which moves artificiall Wings made to beat the Aire, much after the fashion of a Bird's flight.' The purpose of his writings was to prove the 'inferiority and indignity of magical power' compared with nature and science, in an age of alchemists. He admitted that he had never seen the instrument of flying to which he referred, but was 'exceedingly acquainted with a very prudent man, who hath invented the whole Artifice'.

Bacon was, so far as we know, the first person ever to write about flying in any mechanical or scientific sense. Some later writers claim that he also foresaw the lighter-than-air balloon and airship by conceiving 'a large hollow globe . . . filled with ethereal air . . . which would float on the atmosphere as a ship floats on water'; but there is considerable doubt that he did write this.

Remarkable as Bacon's views were, they fell far short of the genius of a man who was born some two hundred years later – the artist-inventor Leonardo da Vinci, who is best remembered for his painting of the *Mona Lisa*. In our scientific age it is impossible to appreciate the true greatness of this man, whose sketchbooks contain designs for winged flying apparatus, helicopters and parachutes, produced in an age of crossbows and soldiers in armour. He observed closely the flight of birds, realising that it was not only the shape of their wings but the way in which they used them that enabled them to fly under all conditions.

Leonardo da Vinci's aircraft, like his embryo submarines and tanks, were far too advanced for a backward age, and in the centuries that followed flying remained exclusive to the birds, while bird-men flapped and died amid the wood and feather debris of their wings, and sixteenth- and seventeenth-century science fiction writers like Bishop Godwin and Cyrano de Bergerac wrote about men on the moon, and journeys to that satellite in such fanciful spaceships as glass balls containing dew which rose when subjected to the sun's rays.

It was another ecclesiastic scholar – Bishop Wilkins (1614–72) – who kept the theory of flying on more practical lines in his *Discourse concerning the possibility of a passage to the World in the Moon* and *Mathematical Magick*. He still thought mainly in terms of flying with bird-like wings, but realised that man's arms were not strong enough by themselves, and suggested using the legs as well – as had Leonardo da Vinci, whose works were to remain largely unknown until 1797. He also made a major step forward by discussing the possibility of a 'flying chariot', going into details such as the length, breadth, strength and weight of the wings, the necessity of providing some sort of control and even mechanical propulsion.

As a variation on the bird-man theme, a French locksmith named Besnier tried to fly in 1678 with the aid of four hinged flaps or wings fixed to the ends of two rods and worked over the shoulders by both arms and legs. He had no more success than John Damian, who, stepping out of the wreckage of wings with which he had tried to fly to France from Stirling Castle, had the presence of mind to blame his failure on the use of feathers from chickens, which are ground birds, instead of eagles' feathers.

Little wonder that, by the start of the seventeenth century, would-be airmen began to turn their attention to lighter-than-air flight, rather than wings. Several people, notably Francisco di Mendoza and three Jesuits – Laureto Lauro, Athanasius Kircher, and Gaspard Schott – began to realise that if a body could be made lighter than air it would float in the air; and this led in 1670 to the ingenious 'flying boat' of the inventive Jesuit priest Francesco de Lana-Terzi.

It obviously owed a lot to Otto van Guericke's air pump, invented twenty years earlier, the general idea being to lift a boat-shaped carriage into the air by means of four large copper globes from which all the air had been extracted. De Lana calculated that if the copper were thin enough the globes would be considerably lighter than the air they displaced and would, therefore, float. Unfortunately, it proved completely impossible to build globes of sufficient size and lightness that would also be strong enough to withstand atmospheric pressure. At which point de Lana said that he did not want to build any flying machines anyway, in case they were used to drop boiling oil and other unpleasant commodities onto armies at war.

On 8th August 1709 the Brazilian priest Bartolomeu de Gusmão demonstrated a remarkable model hot-air balloon before King John V of Portugal. Its small paper envelope was inflated with hot air from 'fire material contained in an earthen bowl' suspended beneath it. The balloon rose 12 feet before being destroyed by two valets who thought it might set the curtains alight. The *Passarola* (Great Bird), long thought to be a fantastic flying machine devised by Gusmão, was simply an artist's conception of the carriage designed for a full-size version of the balloon.

Despite many weird and wonderful projects, the eighteenth century was destined to see man's dream of flight begin to come true. Knowing nothing of Gusmão's experiments, Joseph Galien, without explaining how, proposed in 1755 to fill with rarefied air from high above the earth a vast machine large enough to transport a whole army from his home town of Avignon to Africa. But it was an Englishman, Henry Cavendish, who paved the way for practical lighter-than-air flight in 1766 by discovering that 'inflammable air' – hydrogen – was much lighter than Galien's unprocurable rarefied air.

However, it was not hydrogen but hot air that first lifted a man from the earth in 1783. The story, perhaps improved with age, is that one day, whilst sitting by the fire, the brothers Joseph and Etienne Montgolfier of Annonay, near Lyons, noticed hot air rising above the fire and wondered if it would be sufficiently powerful to lift a paper bag. It was, so they tried it with bigger bags – they were paper-makers, which helped – and then, on 4th June, 1783, with a 110-foot-circumference spherical balloon made of paper-lined linen which rose to about 6,000 feet before a large crowd when inflated with common air heated by means of a fire.

Other successes followed fast. On 19th September the first living creatures ever to leave the ground in an aircraft – a sheep, a cock and a duck – travelled almost two miles in a wicker basket slung under a *Montgolfière* released at Versailles. There could be only one sequel, and it was planned to carry under the next balloon a criminal who would receive a free pardon if he alighted safely.

But a young scientist named Pilâtre de Rozier, considering it unthinkable that a criminal should gain the honour of being the first airman, volunteered to make the ascent himself; and on 15th October 1783 he rose to about 80 feet in a captive balloon with a capacity of 60,000 cu. ft. More important, on 21st November he completed the first aerial voyage in history, with the Marquis d'Arlandes, by flying $5\frac{1}{2}$ miles across Paris at a height of up to 1,500 feet, from

10

the Château de la Muette. The 25-minute flight was not without hazard, for the balloon was kept inflated with hot air by means of a brazier slung under its neck, and the airman had a hectic time putting out fires on the fabric with a sponge and water which they had wisely decided to take with them.

To the hot-air balloon, therefore, goes the credit of proving human flight possible; but it did not survive for long. The early successes of the Montgolfiers had prompted the geologist Faujas de Saint-Fond to raise a public subscription for construction of a small silk hydrogen-filled balloon by J.-A.-C. Charles, the physicist, and two mechanics, the brothers Robert. This balloon flew 15 miles, unpiloted, on 27th August 1783; and on 1st December Charles and the elder Robert flew for more than two hours in a 26-foot-diameter hydrogen balloon, from the Tuileries Gardens in Paris, some 27 miles to Nesle. After touching down, Charles went up again by himself, but was so alarmed when the balloon shot up to over 9,000 feet that he never flew again.

More important than the flights themselves was the fact that Charles's balloon was such a masterpiece of design and manufacture that many of its features – the valve, the net, the suspension of the basket, the provision of ballast, use of a barometer and, of course, the gas – have been retained to this day in free balloons.

The sport of ballooning, in both hot-air *Montgolfières* and hydrogen-filled *Charlières*, spread rapidly. The first woman aeronaut, Mme Tible, ascended from Lyons as passenger in a *Montgolfière* in June 1784. The first successful flight in Italy had occurred four months earlier, and on 25th August the first brief ascent in Great Britain was made at Edinburgh by James Tytler. The first aerial voyage in England followed on 15th September, when a young Italian named Vincenzo Lunardi flew 25 miles from the Artillery Ground, Moorfields, to Ware in Hertfordshire, before touring with his balloon to Liverpool, Edinburgh, Glasgow, York and Newcastle.

Lunardi and the Frenchman J.-P. Blanchard soon became the greatest of the early aeronauts; and on 7th January 1785 the latter showed England for the first time that she was no longer wholly protected by her moat, by crossing the Channel from Dover to the Forest of Guines, 12 miles inland from Calais, in a hydrogen balloon with the American Dr. Jeffries, who put up the cash for the attempt. It was not an easy crossing; the balloon began to lose height so rapidly at one stage that the airmen had to throw overboard everything they could lay their hands on to lighten it, including their trousers and a bottle of good French brandy!

Ballooning quickly became a popular spectacle, and Blanchard travelled to Ghent, Breslau, Prague, Warsaw, Vienna and even the United States in the next eight years to give demonstration flights – often the first flights made in each country. Sometimes the balloonists were accompanied by parachutists, after André-Jacques Garnerin had made the first successful jump from a balloon on 22nd October 1797, over Paris. An Englishman named Robert Cocking tried to improve on Garnerin's design, which sometimes swayed so violently that its inventor was sick, but he fell to his death when it collapsed during its trials in July 1837. In fact the list of fatalities grew fairly rapidly, which added to the interest from a spectator's viewpoint!

First aeronaut to fly – Pilâtre de Rozier – had also been the first to die, on 15th June 1785. He was attempting to cross the Channel in a balloon using both hot air and hydrogen. The combination of fire and highly inflammable gas could

Lighter than Air

7. (*Left*) The first aeronauts, a sheep, a cock and a duck, flew 2 miles in a *Montgolfière* hot-air balloon on 19th September 1783.

8. (*Right*) Start of the first aerial journey in history – a 5½-mile flight over Paris by Pilâtre de Rozier and the Marquis d'Arlandes in a *Montgolfière* on 21st November 1783.

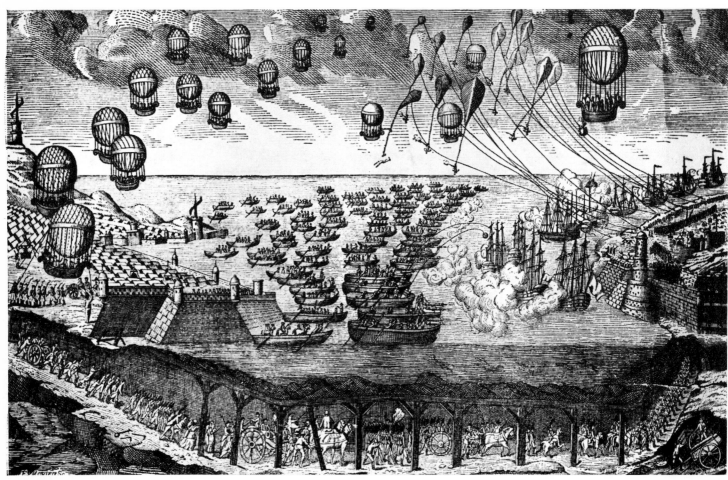

9. Invasion of Britain. To by-pass the Royal Navy Napoleon studied every possibility from a Channel tunnel to use of huge *Montgolfière* balloons, each carrying 3,000 troops.

10. (*Left*) Leonardo da Vinci invented the parachute; but not until the balloon had been perfected was the first successful parachute descent made by Garnerin, in 1797. This print shows him making the first descent in England in 1802, over North Audley Street, London.

11. (*Above*) First of the airships – Giffard's steam-powered aircraft in which, in 1852, he flew from Paris to Trappes at 6 m.p.h.

12. The electrically-driven *La France*, built in 1884, was the first completely practical airship, able to be steered in flight in any direction, irrespective of wind. It was 165 feet long and had a speed of $14\frac{1}{2}$ m.p.h.

13. Not until the petrol engine was invented could airships be given a reasonable performance. Outstanding among the pioneers was Santos-Dumont, who first fitted a petrol engine to an airship in 1898, eight years before he achieved even greater fame with the first official aeroplane flight in Europe.

have only one result, and both de Rozier and his passenger died when their balloon caught fire near Boulogne.

Chief disadvantage of balloons was that they were completely at the mercy of the elements. Man was, in fact, still a very long way from flying like the birds, for the balloon could best be likened to a boat in mid-ocean, without oars, sail, rudder or engine. Blanchard tried to provide some measure of control by the use of oars and little windmill propellers called *moulinets*, without success; and flying seemed likely to remain little more than a hazardous sport and spectacle.

A few military uses were found for captive balloons, an outstanding operation being on 26th June 1794 when Captain Coutelle made ascents totalling several hours during the Battle of Fleurus in Belgium. The information he signalled down to General Jourdan's Moselle army contributed greatly to the important victory which the French forces gained over the Allies; and Coutelle repeated his performance soon afterwards when the French defeated the Austrians on the Ourthe, near Liege.

As a result the 'Company of Aérostiers' was enlarged and a new-type cylindrical balloon put into service. But aerial reconnaissance proved of little use when attempted during the siege of Mayence and elsewhere, and the Aérostiers were disbanded in 1799. Needless to say, the British Army refused to have anything to do with the new-fangled ideas until more than sixty years later, by which time the Austrians had attacked Venice with pilotless bomb-carrying *Montgolfières* in 1849 – nearly a hundred years before Hitler's V.1 flying bomb – and McClellan's Federal army had achieved a certain amount of success with captive reconnaissance balloons in the American Civil War.

In 1862 Henry Coxwell was commissioned to undertake a series of experiments at Aldershot, using captive balloons of 50,000 cu. ft. capacity for reconnaissance, signalling and to drop high explosive on the enemy – a technique he had been the first to demonstrate, in Berlin, in 1848. But the Army were still little interested, and Coxwell eventually left for Germany to instruct two balloon detachments at Cologne, at the start of the Franco-German War of 1870.

His trainees met with little more success than the French in military operations; but the latter operated a thriving civilian balloon service during the siege of Paris in 1870. Sixty-six balloons left the city, mostly by night, carrying more than a 100 V.I.P. refugees, 9 tons of mail and over 400 carrier pigeons. Only 7 of them failed to reach safety; and the 57 pigeons that managed to find their way back to the city carried in about 100,000 messages on microfilm – an idea we re-invented as the Airgraph letter to save space on our mailplanes in World War II.

Chief disadvantages of the military balloons were that they had to be accompanied by a heavy generator, acid cart and other gear, took some three hours to inflate and were difficult to control in a high wind. The last disadvantage was finally overcome in 1897 by a German officer named von Parseval, who designed the sausage-shaped *Drachen* kite-balloon, with tail-fins to keep it pointed into wind. Later, compressed gas in cylinders eased transport and inflation problems, and the kite-balloon was widely used by both sides in the 1914–18 War. It was fairly vulnerable, however, and by World War II the captive balloon survived only in the anti-aircraft balloon barrage, bringing down, in addition to enemy warplanes, 232 flying-bombs over southern England in 1944–5.

Militarily, therefore, balloons have had their day; and very few survive as sporting aircraft. But they have been used for 170 years for scientific research, and free pilotless balloons are still being released every day to collect meteorological data and secrets of the upper atmosphere. The earliest ascent for scientific purposes was in November 1784 when Blanchard and Dr. Jeffries brought back samples of the upper air for analysis by Henry Cavendish. More significant were the flights made in 1803–4 by Etienne Robertson and Gay-Lussac, which proved that neither magnetic force nor the composition of the air varied at heights up to 22,000 feet.

Little more was done until the mid-century. Then, in 1859, the British Association organised the most important series of scientific balloon ascents ever made in Britain. Heights of 20,000 feet were reached on several occasions by Henry Coxwell and James Glaisher, who, on 5th September 1862, had the terrifying experience of climbing to (they claimed) about 37,000 feet before the nearly-insensible Coxwell managed to pull the valve-line to release some of the gas and descend. As a point of interest, this height was not reached by an aeroplane until 1927, and the official world height record of 72,395 feet was still held by a free balloon – the 3,700,000 cu. ft. American *Explorer II* – thirty years later rocket-powered research aircraft have climbed considerably higher.

But the limitations of free balloons had been realised right from the start. Blanchard's oars and windmills were completely ineffective, and the balloon remained at the mercy of the elements. Some remarkable flights were achieved with a back wind – Charles Green, first to use coal-gas instead of hydrogen, made a remarkable flight of 480 miles to Weilburg in Germany in November 1836; and John Wise flew 1,120 miles from St. Louis to Henderson, New York, in 1859. But there was no question of return tickets unless the wind changed; and everyone realised that what was needed was a self-propelled, steerable balloon – a true air-ship.

Oars, wings, sails, rudders, teams of trained eagles – all these, and others, were suggested and rejected in turn. So were jets of steam and rockets. More practical was the airscrew tested in 1784 by Blanchard; but, manually turned, it produced totally insufficient thrust to counteract the wind. What was needed was an engine of some sort – and it was destined to be needed for a very long time!

Gen. Meusnier suggested that airships ought to be elongated in shape; but the greatest of all the early pioneers was an Englishman, Sir George Cayley, who discovered the basic principle of aeronautics that led in turn to both the navigable balloon and the aeroplane.

This man, the 'Father of British Aeronautics', was born at Brompton Hall, Yorkshire, in 1773. At the age of 10 he heard about the first balloon flights in France and, after that, never lost his enthusiasm for flying. In 1796 he experimented with a Chinese flying-top toy, which incorporates the principle of both the airscrew and helicopter rotor. Then, by fitting a cruciform tail to a kite he built the first practical glider, establishing the positions of wings and tail as on a modern aircraft. It was the first fixed-wing aeroplane in the world to fly, but not the first heavier-than-air craft, as Launoy and Bienvenu had flown a model helicopter, with two four-bladed rotors made of feathers, in 1784. By 1808 Cayley's small model had been developed into a glider bigger than a Spitfire, and rumour has it that he made his reluctant coachman fly 300 yards across a valley in a later aircraft, after which the old man resigned on the spot.

15

We have no proof that this story is true; but we have plenty of proof of Cayley's later contributions to the science of flight. Like Leonardo da Vinci, he studied the birds, and deduced that aircraft wings ought to be cambered. He added that a braced biplane wing would combine high lift with a structural strength, and designed an aircraft to prove his theories; but he then abandoned the whole thing in favour of airships, which he considered more useful as potential passenger-carriers.

Cayley, like Meusnier, advocated a proper streamlined gas-bag, and his airship project of 1837 also introduced steam-driven propellers for propulsion and steering. But it was not built, and it was left to another Frenchman, Pierre Jullien, to build the first successful airship – a clockwork-powered, streamlined model named the *Précurseur* – in 1850. It paved the way for the first full-size airship of Henri Giffard, which in 1852 flew from Paris to Trappes at the reckless speed of 6 m.p.h. It was fitted with a 3-h.p. steam engine and was only partly controllable; but that does not lessen Giffard's importance in the forefront of aviation pioneers, with the Montgolfiers, Cayley, and the Wright Brothers.

Despite Giffard's success, he did not entirely set the fashion for airships. When Paul Haenlein of Germany put the unofficial speed record up to 10 m.p.h. in 1872, his airship was driven by an engine fed with gas from the envelope, and in America Professor Richell built a tiny, virtually-uncontrolled airship with a pedal-driven propeller. The first completely successful airship, able to be steered in flight back to its starting point, irrespective of wind, was the electrically-driven *La France*, built in 1884 by Renard and Krebs.

It only remained for the little Brazilian pioneer Alberto Santos-Dumont to fit a petrol engine to an airship in 1898 and, later, to prove its capabilities by flying round the Eiffel Tower – an exploit which won him 100,000 (1901-type) francs. The airship had arrived.

It did not take the German Armed Services long to realise the military significance of an aerial ship able to travel anywhere under its own power. Count von Zeppelin began to plan a series of giant military airships as early as 1874 – not merely elongated balloons like the 'blimps' and semi-rigid airships then flying, but real flying ships, built around a rigid metal framework. The first aircraft of this type was completed by his compatriot Schwarz in 1897, but it was Zeppelin's airships that were destined to become in time among the most feared and, later, most respected aircraft ever built.

The first was begun in 1898 and completed two years later. On its second flight it buckled so severely that the Count could not afford to repair it, and that would have been the end of the Zeppelins had he not been allowed to hold a State lottery to raise the cash for another. This one too was wrecked in a gale. Undismayed, he held more lotteries and built more airships, eventually achieving such success that the Zeppelin became a symbol of German air power.

But by that time there were even more significant shapes in the sky, thanks to the availability of the petrol engine – the power plant that would-be airmen had sought for so long.

Once again the story really begins with Sir George Cayley, whose glider and theories about rigid wings had almost killed the old preference for flapping wings. He also designed a remarkable convertiplane[1]; but this did not influence

[1] A convertiplane, nowadays, is an aircraft which takes off as a helicopter and converts into an autogiro or fixed-wing aeroplane for cruising flight.

his successors as much as his earlier work, which was just as well! Most of those successors were English, because the French concentrated their efforts on balloons and airships in the nineteenth century.

The problems that faced would-be aviators (heavier-than-air) were the same as those which had confronted the aeronauts (lighter-than-air) – first to find a way of getting into the air and staying there, then to perfect control, stability and means of propulsion.

First came William Samuel Henson (born 1805), who, in 1842, designed a most remarkable Aerial Steam Carriage, based on Cayley's theories and his own experiments with model gliders. Together with another enthusiast named John Stringfellow, he built a 20-foot model of it, and this can still be seen in the National Aeronautical Collection at South Kensington. It never flew; but in many respects was far more logical than some of the full-scale aircraft that did totter into the air sixty years later. Its design, with fuselage slung under its monoplane wing, a tail, nosewheel undercarriage and two pusher propellers, is in fact basically the same as that of a conventional aeroplane of today.

Unfortunately, Henson let his enthusiasm run riot. He issued imaginative colour drawings of the aircraft in flight over London, Paris and even the Pyramids; at the same time trying to get Parliament to pass a Bill authorising the setting up of an Aerial Steam Transit Company to operate world-wide air services with steam carriages. Not unnaturally, the whole idea was greeted with hoots of derision by Parliament and Press alike, so Henson lost heart and went to America.

Stringfellow decided to carry on alone, and began by designing a steam engine that would be light enough yet powerful enough to lift an aeroplane. Having overcome this major barrier to powered flight, he fitted the engine to a 10-foot model based on the Steam Carriage, and it was an accepted fact for many years that this model became the first heavier-than-air powered aeroplane to fly, at Chard in Somerset, in 1848. Now, in the absence of any contemporary reports of a successful free flight, and after studying correspondence between Stringfellow and other persons, historians dispute this claim. Nor is String-fellow thought to have achieved any greater success with a model triplane that he demonstrated in 1868 at the first Aeronautical Exhibition organised at the Crystal Palace by the (later Royal) Aeronautical Society of Great Britain, which had been formed two years earlier. Indeed, his chief claim to a place in aviation history seems to be as a craftsman in the construction of small steam engines, for apparently he knew nothing about controls and sacrificed all ideas of strength to get a light model into which to put his engines.

A far less controversial figure was Francis Wenham, who at the first meeting of the Aeronautical Society in 1866 read a paper on 'Aerial Locomotion' which confirmed Cayley's beliefs and laid down almost every basic principle on which the theory and practice of heavier-than-air flight are founded. He also made the first wind-tunnel experiments in 1871.

There were still plenty of completely impractical designs. Werner von Siemens in Germany designed a crescent-wing rocket-plane, and there were flapping-wing creations in plenty; but, in general, aviation began to advance.

Thomas Moy tested his huge Aerial Steamer, tied to a circular track, at Crystal Palace in 1875, and claimed that it left the ground briefly. Four years earlier Alphonse Pénaud in France had built a little rubber-powered model which proved so successful that he scaled it up into a full-size aeroplane. The

Towards the Aeroplane

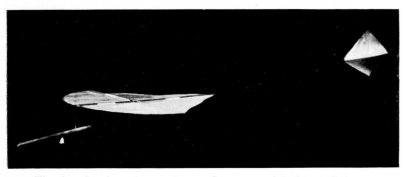

14. First heavier-than-air aeroplane to fly was a model glider built in 1804 by Sir George Cayley. It was little more than a 154 sq. in. kite mounted on a rod, with a tail at the rear.

15. Cayley's 'Aerial Carriage' of 1843 had four rotating wings which opened out like eight-bladed ship's propellers when required for lifting, and two pusher propellers.

16. A drawing of Henson's proposed Aerial Steam Carriage – the first design for a complete powered aeroplane.

17. Replica of John Stringfellow's 1848 steam-powered monoplane, which until recently was credited with having made the first flight by a

heavier-than-air powered aeroplane. Developed from Henson's Aerial Steam Carriage, it was launched down a 30-foot-long inclined wire, a stop being used to release the model from its carriage.

18. Although the Wright brothers are generally recognised as first to make a controlled and sustained flight in a powered aeroplane, they have several challengers. In about 1874 a Frenchman named Felix Du Temple built a steam-powered monoplane which made a short hop at Brest, after taking off down an inclined ramp. This was probably the first-ever flight by a powered man-carrying aeroplane, but it would not have been possible without the assistance of the ramp. The same is true of I. N. Golubev's 1882 hop in the steam-powered aeroplane designed by Alexander Mozhaisky (*right*), as he also took off down a steep slope. Nevertheless, Russia still claims this as the first proper powered flight.

19–20. Sir Hiram Maxim achieved a little success in 1894 with the fantastic structure of steel tube and canvas shown on the right. It weighed 3½ tons, spanned 104 feet and was powered by two 180-h.p. steam engines, one of which Sir Hiram is carrying in the photograph above. His aircraft lifted itself from the ground but was not controllable.

21. Clement Ader of France is said to have flown 150 feet in this bat-like *Eole* monoplane on 9th October 1890. But the flight was almost certainly uncontrolled. *Eole* had a wing-span of 46 feet, weighed 1,100 lb. and was powered by a 20-h.p. steam engine. Ader sat inside its fuselage and tried to control it by flexing the wings.

22. The Australian pioneer Lawrence Hargrave built several successful compressed-air-driven models, with both airscrews and flapping wings. More important, he invented the cellular box-kite structure which formed the basis of many early powered aircraft.

23. Otto Lilienthal with one of the beautiful bird-like gliders in which he made more than two thousand successful flights in the 1890s.

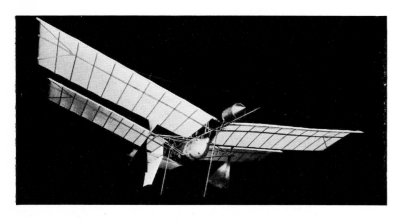

24–7. In 1896 Dr. Samuel Pierpont Langley flew successfully the 16-foot-span tandem-wing model shown above. Powered by a 2-h.p. steam engine, it covered 3,200 feet at 25 m.p.h. Seven years later he completed a full-size version of this 'Aerodrome', as he called it, powered by a remarkable 52-h.p. five-cylinder radial engine designed by Charles Manly. In its first test, piloted by Manly (below), it hit a post on the launching track, which was mounted on a houseboat, and crashed into the Potomac River. Two months later, on 8th December 1903 (right), it again met with disaster when its rear wings and tail collapsed during launching.

result was by far the most advanced design conceived up to that time, but Pénaud had not the money to build it. If he had, and if there had been a suitable engine for it, he might well have been the first man to fly.

Many pioneers followed the lead of Henson, Stringfellow, Moy and company by falling back on the steam engine in the absence of anything better. The Russians, in fact, claim that their Mr. Mozhaisky flew successfully in a big monoplane with three steam-driven propellers in 1884. But the claim is not recognised outside Russia.

There have been plenty of other claimants for the title of first to fly in a powered aeroplane, one of the foremost being the Frenchman Clement Ader (1841–1925). Indeed there is little doubt that he did leave the ground for a brief moment in his weird, bat-like monoplane *L'Eole* on 9th October 1890; but it could have been no more than an uncontrolled hop, although witnesses say it flew for 50 yards. Later, in 1897, Ader made a further series of tests with his *Avion III*, which was financed by the French War Department; but, looking at its design now, it was perhaps as well for the future of aviation that this gallant gentleman just failed.

In England the great American-born scientist Sir Hiram Maxim also made a brief uncontrolled flight in 1894 in a fantastic contraption of wings, wires and windmills, bigger than a Lancaster bomber of World War II. Powered by two 180-h.p. steam engines, it weighed $3\frac{1}{2}$ tons and was built solely to test Sir Hiram's theories on flying. The last thing the old gentleman wanted to do was to leave the ground in it, so he built a special railway testing track at Bexley in Kent, with guard rails to prevent the aircraft rising more than 2 feet. Despite which, its vast wings developed so much lift when he opened up the engines that the aircraft broke free of its guard rail and flew freely before crashing. It lacked any sort of effective flying controls, so this failure too can be regarded as providential for the science of flight.

It was obvious that the first true powered aeroplane flight could not be delayed much longer. It came not through the headlong achievements of men like Ader, Mozhaisky and Maxim, but as a result of the more gradual methods of a new generation of bird-men – men of genius and patience, who tackled the problem from an engineering or scientific viewpoint, studying the birds, trying not merely to build a contraption that would fly, but to find out what made flying possible and then translate their findings into a simple structure; whilst waiting for the right kind of engine.

It was left to the bird-men – the glider-makers Lilienthal, Pilcher, Chanute, Montgomery, Wilbur and Orville Wright and others – to turn into reality the dream of Pénaud and countless pioneers. Otto Lilienthal the German was first, his contribution being to prove beyond any shadow of doubt that human flight was possible in a heavier-than-air craft. From an artificial hill, he made more than two thousand successful flights in his beautiful bird-like gliders of peeled willow wands covered with waxed cotton cloth. Carefully tabulating the results of his tests, he gradually improved the design, achieving flights of a quarter of a mile at heights up to 75 feet. But he made the fatal mistake of relying on movement of his body in the air to control the aircraft's flight; and on 9th August 1896, at the age of 48, he lost control, crashed and died.

His 'disciples' Percy Pilcher in England, and Octave Chanute in America, carried on where Lilienthal had ended, with considerable success: and an Australian, Lawrence Hargrave, perfected the box-kite, which was due to play a great part in the development of aviation in the pioneer days. Equally important, Chanute wrote a book entitled *Progress in Flying Machines* in which he collated all worthwhile data on aeronautical design up to that time. This book and the achievements of Otto Lilienthal provided the vital spark which kindled an interest in aviation in Wilbur and Orville Wright, two young bicycle makers of Dayton, Ohio.

No reckless do-or-die would-be airmen, they first learned all they could about the successes and failures of others, and soon realised that the major problems were to achieve stability and control in the air. Finding a suitable engine could come later, and might not be so difficult now that the petrol engine had been invented.

They built a glider which they tested in 1900 by flying it mainly as a kite at the end of ropes. It was controlled by a forward elevator and warping wingtips, very similar in function to modern ailerons, and proved quite successful. In the following year they produced another glider which should have been better – but was not. Disappointed, they went home and built a wind tunnel from an old starch box, in which they tested scores of tiny model wings. The reason for their failure was apparent in the tables of test results, which showed that almost every scrap of data on wing design produced by their predecessors was inaccurate. So they started from scratch and built another glider with wings of completely new section. It worked after being fitted with a moveable rudder, and they made about a thousand flights in it in September and October 1902.

After three and a half years of patient hard work, scientific reasoning and sheer determination, Wilbur and Orville now felt the time was right to build a powered version of their latest successful design. They were quite confident that, when completed, it would fly; but did not regard this fact as anything of world-shattering importance, merely another milestone in their development of a practical aeroplane.

So the 17th December 1903 found them back at the isolated settlement of Kitty Hawk in North Carolina, where they had made their gliding experiments. It was little more than a tiny name on a very large map. A score of houses dotted the countryside a mile from the strip of sandy beach, where the only signs of life were a government weather bureau, life-saving station, and a small group of men clustered round the contraption of stick, string and canvas which the Wrights called, somewhat optimistically, their flying machine.

Nine days earlier Charles Manly had attempted to fly from a houseboat on the Potomac River in a tandem-wing aircraft designed by Dr. Samuel Pierpont Langley, secretary of the Smithsonian Institution. Named the *Aerodrome*, this machine was a scaled-up petrol-engined version of a small steam-powered model flown with great success by Langley in 1896, and had been financed to the extent of $50,000 by the U.S. War Department. Unfortunately, its rear wing and tail were damaged as it left its launching catapult, and it plunged straight into the river. So the coast was now clear for Wilbur and Orville Wright.

28. The photographs on this page symbolise the reasons why the Wright brothers succeeded where so many other would-be aviators had failed. Realising the first essentials were to achieve stability and control, they first tested their ideas with pilotless gliders which they flew as kites.

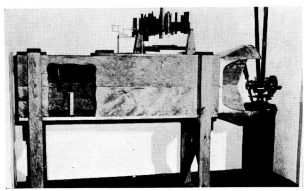

29–30. Not until they had developed new wing sections with the help of their primitive wind tunnel (*right*) and made more than a thousand flights with their 1901 and 1902 gliders (*below*) – so successfully that they set up several distance records – did the Wrights attempt to build a powered aircraft.

A few minutes before eleven o'clock Orville lay down on the lower wing of his aircraft, started its home-made engine and, after a few minutes, released a wire which held it to a metal track. As it lumbered forward into the 27-knot wind, Wilbur ran alongside, holding a wing-tip to balance it.

Suddenly, it rose into the air, and one of the life-saving men took this photograph of the start of the first controlled and sustained flight by a powered aeroplane in history – the fulfilment of man's centuries-old dream of flying with the birds.

It was not much of a flight by modern standards – Orville covered only 120 feet – less than the wing span of many modern air liners. His speed was only 31 m.p.h. and the flight lasted just 12 seconds. But from such modest beginnings have come wings to lift a world.

Years of Trial and Error

ORVILLE and Wilbur Wright made three more flights on 17th December 1903, covering a distance of 852 feet in 59 seconds on the last one. It should have been the story of a lifetime for the American Press; yet only a handful of newspapers found room for a garbled, half-sceptical report of the experiments at Kitty Hawk.

Unperturbed, the brothers continued to improve their aeroplane. A falling-weight catapult was designed to speed take-off. The controls were changed so that the pilot could sit down instead of having to lie on the wing. Stability, control and power were improved; and eventually the Wrights realised they had a machine that offered tremendous possibilities for military reconnaissance duties. So they offered it to the U.S. Army; only to be told on 24th October 1905 that the Board of Ordnance and Fortification 'does not care to formulate any requirements for the performance of a flying machine or take any further action on the subject until a machine is produced which by actual operation is shown to be able to produce horizontal flight and to carry an operator'.

Nineteen days earlier, in their best flight of the year, they had covered $24\frac{1}{5}$ miles in 38 minutes 3 seconds! But if the U.S. Government was not interested other countries were. Colonel J. E. Capper of H.M. Balloon Factory at Farnborough travelled personally to America to invite the brothers to continue their work in England; only to learn on his return that the Treasury would not provide the necessary finance. Yet this was a blessing in disguise, because it compelled the factory to rely on its own resources and led eventually to official support for two of our greatest pioneers – S. F. Cody and J. W. Dunne.

The Wrights were not worried when their initial sales campaign failed, because there was no evidence that anyone else in the world had achieved a proper controlled flight of even a few yards in a powered aeroplane. There were plenty of rumours. For example, Karl Jatho of Hanover, Germany, said that he had flown 24 kilometres in his biplane on 18th August 1903. The Hungarian designer Trajan Vuia was said to have hopped a dozen yards or so near Paris on 18th March 1906; and to this day many people acknowledge J. C. H. Ellehammer of Denmark as the first to fly in Europe because of a reported 42-metre hop made on 12th September 1906.

Surprisingly, one of the most genuine claims did not come to light until 1953, when J. Y. Watson of Blairgowrie, Scotland, stated that his brother, Preston Watson, had flown successfully in 1902 in an ingenious biplane fitted with a Santos-Dumont engine. It is virtually impossible to confirm such claims after fifty years; but Preston Watson deserves a place among the great pioneers of flight.

With so many claimants and no general agreement on what constitutes a proper controlled, sustained flight, it is hardly surprising that the question of who was first to fly has never been settled to everyone's satisfaction. Even in America the Wrights' claim was disputed for many years because, in an attempt

26

to disprove their patent rights, Glenn Curtiss rebuilt the Langley *Aerodrome* in 1914 and flew it as a seaplane. According to the Smithsonian Institution, this proved that Langley preceded the Wrights as designer of the first practical aeroplane. Not until 1942 would they admit that the *Aerodrome's* 1914 flights were possible only because Glenn Curtiss made important changes in its design.

The Wrights never doubted their monopoly in powered flight, and on 10th October 1906 Wilbur wrote to a friend: 'We do not believe there is one chance in a hundred that anyone will have a machine of the least practical usefulness within five years.'

Less than a fortnight later Santos-Dumont flew 60 metres in France. His aeroplane was primitive; but it proved the practicability of flight to a continent that was still sceptical and paved the way for better designs – better even than the Wright biplane. From that moment France began to become the centre of world aviation progress.

Outstanding among French designers were the Voisin brothers, and it was on one of their biplanes, in January 1908, that Henry Farman made the first circular flight of 1 kilometre in Europe, to win a prize of 50,000 francs.

Such prizes were responsible for much of the progress made in Europe at that time. Few of the pioneers were rich men and fewer still could count on any form of government subsidy. So aviation owes much to men like the late Lord Northcliffe, who had such faith in the future of flying that in 1906 he offered, through his newspaper the *Daily Mail*, a series of prizes ranging from £250 for model aircraft to £1,000 for the first airman to fly the English Channel and £10,000 for the first to fly from London to Manchester in 24 hours. At once the editor of a rival newspaper wrote sarcastically that he would give £10 *million* to anyone who could fly between the two cities.

Nevertheless aviation made rapid progress. In England A. V. Roe won part of the *Daily Mail* prize for model aircraft and used it to build an aeroplane at Brooklands, although he had to go without food to pay for the hire of its engine. Like other British pioneers, he was regarded by officials and public alike as a mixture of menace and candidate for the nearest padded cell. Because of this attitude many of our finest pilots did their flying in France; which explains why English-born Henry Farman earned his reputation as the first great European airman flying French aeroplanes.

On 30th October 1908 he made the first cross-country flight, from Chalons to Rheims, a distance of 16½ miles, in a Voisin biplane. By then the Wright brothers were flying up to an hour at a time; yet Farman's modest achievement was more significant than theirs, for the French aircraft had wheels and could fly to and from anywhere, whereas the Wright biplane needed its catapult to get it airborne.

So when Wilbur visited France with one of his biplanes the French were impressed and inspired to even greater efforts, yet had the courage and fore-sight to develop their own designs rather than merely to copy the Wright machine. The Voisin brothers built up a thriving production line of their biplanes. Louis Blériot, Leon Levavasseur and Robert Esnault-Pelterie, by a long, expensive, dangerous process of trial and error, developed a new shape – the monoplane. And it was one of these aircraft that, on 25th July 1909, won the first great *Daily Mail* prize of £1,000 by crossing the English Channel and proving that, for good or evil, the aeroplane would in future recognise no barriers of frontier or ocean.

32. There is still no general agreement on who was first to fly an aeroplane in Europe. One of the earliest British pioneers was a young Scotsman named Preston Watson, who first built and flew a Wright-type glider. Later he produced a succession of aircraft, like this glider, which were controlled by tilting the pivoted top wing; but it is doubtful if any of these flew before 1910.

33. Many people still accept the claim of J. C. H. Ellehammer of Denmark, who built his first aircraft in 1904 and tested it extensively in tethered flight on the island of Lindholm.

34. On 12th September 1906 Ellehammer is reported to have flown this aeroplane for 42 metres at a height of about 20 inches above the ground.

35. A reconstructed photograph of the officially- recognised first flight in Europe, made by the little Brazilian Alberto Santos-Dumont at Bagatelle, France, on 23rd October 1906. He flew 60 metres in his tail-first '14 bis' box-bite. On 12th November of the same year he made a further flight of 220 metres and set up the first official air speed record of 25·65 m.p.h.

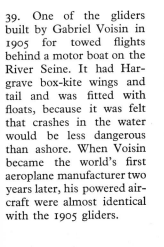

36–7. In England some of the men who later became pace-makers of progress were making a name for themselves in other ways in 1906. The Hon. Charles S. Rolls (*above*), famous motor-racing driver and founder member of the (later Royal) Aero Club of the United Kingdom, was one of the country's leading balloonists. At the Army Balloon Factory at Farnborough, American-born S. F. Cody (*top right*) was busy developing man-lifting kites for military observation duties. One of the most colourful of all airmen, he had once been, like his namesake, Col. 'Buffalo Bill' Cody, a scout and Indian fighter in the Wild West.

38. Trajan Vuia hopped a dozen yards or so on 18th March 1906 in this aircraft, which had folding wings, a 25-h.p. carbonic-acid motor and pneumatic-tyred wheels. Later it hopped 25 yards; but it lacked efficient control and the endurance of its motor was only 3 minutes.

39. One of the gliders built by Gabriel Voisin in 1905 for towed flights behind a motor boat on the River Seine. It had Har-grave box-kite wings and tail and was fitted with floats, because it was felt that crashes in the water would be less dangerous than ashore. When Voisin became the world's first aeroplane manufacturer two years later, his powered air-craft were almost identical with the 1905 gliders.

40. The Marquis d'Equevilley's 12-h.p. flying machine.

41.   Even more fantastic – the Roshon Multiplane.

It was an age of trial and error. If a would-be aviator tried hard enough and long enough, he sometimes achieved the thrill of a short hop. More often a series of errors put him out of business. But even the most fantastic types, like those shown here, contributed something to the new science of aeronautics, and gradually, in France, America and England, more practical aeroplanes began to appear.

42.   One of the first cycle-planes was this patriotically-painted red, white and blue contraption built in 1904 by Monsieur Schmutz.

43. Dapper Monsieur Guillon attempts to make flying history in the Guillon and Clouzy aeroplane, on Epsom Downs on 11th April 1907. The front wheel was the only part of his aircraft to leave the ground.

45. The Bellamy biplane nearing completion.

44. Early enthusiast at Weybridge was bewhiskered Mr. Bellamy, whose big bamboo and canvas gull-wing biplane looked like a frame for growing runner beans.

46. Bellamy's later tailless monoplane, tested at Petersham Meadows in August 1908, was more successful. It did not fly, but taxied quite quickly along the ground!

47. Monsieur Lestage appears to have forgotten the pilot's seat on this multi-rotored helicopter, built in 1907.

48. In France Louis Blériot was more famous for his crashes than for flying. With Voisin's help he built unsuccessful seaplane gliders and powered aircraft with annular wings before making his first hops in this paper-covered tail-first monoplane on 5th April 1907. Its wings folded to save garage space.

49. Horatio Phillips made the important discovery in a form of wind tunnel that a wing with a curved section deflected air upwards, causing a partial vacuum – and lift – over the top surface. Each 'slat' on his venetian blind aircraft was a narrow, curved wing. An early version is said to have flown for 150–250 feet around a circular track at Harrow in 1893, carrying 72 lb. dead weight, but no pilot.

Not until 1908, when the Wrights were flying for periods of up to one hour in America, did anyone fly with confidence in Europe. But, by trial and error methods, French designers made such remarkable progress that their country gradually became the centre of world aviation development. The Voisin brothers built up a thriving production line of their biplanes; and the outstanding aero engines of 1907–9 were undoubtedly Leon Levavasseur's Antoinettes. But perhaps the most significant development in France was the evolution of the monoplane by Blériot, Levavasseur, and Esnault-Pelterie. The absence of struts, and enclosed fuselages of these aircraft represented a colossal advance over the usual 'flying birdcages'.

50. Henry Farman's circular flight of more than 1 kilometre in an Antoinette-powered Voisin biplane, on 13th January 1908, won him a 50,000-franc Deutsch-Archdeacon prize and marked the start of practical flying in Europe. He also made the first cross-country flight, from Chalons to Rheims, a distance of 16½ miles, in another Voisin, on 30th October.

51. Greatest of the early European aviators, Henry Farman was English-born but lived in France, where would-be airmen were treated with more tolerance.

52. Blériot's first completely successful aeroplane was this tandem-wing, Antoinette-powered *Libellule*, in which he flew 25 metres on 11th July 1907, and 184 metres, before crashing, on 17th September. It had rotating wingtip controls.

53. Levavasseur's not very handsome Gastambide-Mengin aircraft led to the later, graceful Antoinette monoplanes, named, like his engines, after M. Gastambide's daughter.

54. Léon Delagrange, another of the great Voisin pilots, who carried the first-ever woman passenger, Mme. Thérèse Peltier, on 8th July 1908.

55. First attempt to produce a low-priced aeroplane that could be assembled and flown safely by anyone and everyone was Santos-Dumont's *Demoiselle*. Built of bamboo and canvas and with a 25-h.p. Darracq motor, it weighed only 242 lb., spanned 18 feet, flew at 60 m.p.h. and could be carried on the back of a truck. Cost was £300, and a fair number were flown without killing anybody.

56. French designers also pioneered vertical take-off with some success. First helicopter to lift itself from the ground carrying a pilot was this Breguet-Richet Gyroplane No. 1, on 29th September 1907: but it was held steady by four assistants. Its 45-h.p. Antoinette engine drove four big rotors, and it weighed 1,275 lb.

57. Paul Cornu's helicopter was first to make a free flight carrying a pilot, on 13th November 1907. Powered by an Antoinette engine, it rose about 1 foot on its first flight, and then climbed to 5 feet carrying Cornu and his brother. Unfortunately, he lacked the money to continue with his experiments.

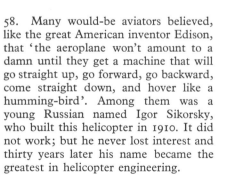

58. Many would-be aviators believed, like the great American inventor Edison, that 'the aeroplane won't amount to a damn until they get a machine that will go straight up, go forward, go backward, come straight down, and hover like a humming-bird'. Among them was a young Russian named Igor Sikorsky, who built this helicopter in 1910. It did not work; but he never lost interest and thirty years later his name became the greatest in helicopter engineering.

59–60. 1908 was the heyday of the Wright brothers' success. Wilbur travelled to France with one of their biplanes, and the confidence and apparent ease of his flying gave new inspiration to the French pioneers. During the year he carried dozens of passengers, flew solo for more than 2 hours 18 minutes without landing, and started a modest flying school. His camp at Pau was visited by hundreds of famous people, including King Edward VII of Great Britain (*below left*).

61–62. While Wilbur was in France Orville was busy in America. In December 1907 the U.S. Army had at last drawn up specifications for an aeroplane and invited tenders. The Wrights' offer of a biplane for $25,000 was accepted, and Orville delivered the aircraft to Fort Myer, Virginia, in the autumn of 1908. After several test flights he set up three endurance records on 9th September, and later took up a number of passengers, including the gentleman shown above, who was probably unimpressed by the very open 'cockpit'. All went well until 17th September, when the biplane crashed from 50 feet, injuring Orville and killing his passenger.

Other events in America showed that the reign of the Wrights was drawing to a close. In 1907 the great Canadian inventor Alexander Graham Bell formed the Aerial Experiment Association. His colleagues were four young men – F. W. Baldwin, Lt. T. E. Selfridge, J. A. D. McCurdy, and Glenn Curtiss, who had designed the engine for the first U.S. military airship in 1905.

63. (*Right*) Glenn Curtiss – greatest of all the American pioneers, after the Wrights.

64. Bell's incredible tetrahedral kite lifted a man, but had so much drag that it was obviously impractical.

65. First powered aeroplane of the Association was the *Red Wing*, designed by Selfridge, who died in the Wright biplane crash at Fort Myer. It was unsuccessful, but paved the way for Baldwin's *White Wing*, which flew 1,017 feet in May 1908.

66. Curtiss's *June Bug*, with a 40-h.p. lightweight V.8 engine of his own design, was outstandingly successful. In it he won a trophy presented by the *Scientific American* magazine on 4th July 1908, with a flight of nearly 1 mile.

Last A.E.A. aeroplane was McCurdy's fine *Silver Dart*, which made more than two hundred flights. After its completion the Association disbanded. Curtiss formed America's earliest aircraft manufacturing company, partnered initially by another pioneer, A. M. Herring. Their first product was the *Gold Bug*, prototype of Curtiss's later highly successful machines and first to be offered for sale to the general public.

67. S. F. Cody, the great American-born pioneer. In 1907 he fitted a 12-h.p. Buchet engine to one of his kites (Fig. 37) and flew it as a pilotless aeroplane. He then obtained War Office permission to build a full-size aeroplane at the Balloon Factory.

68. On 16th October 1908 Cody made the first official aeroplane flight in Britain in his powered biplane, covering 1,390 feet at a height of 50–60 feet over Laffan's Plain, Farnborough. This shows the same aircraft, slightly reconstructed, in 1909.

69–70. Cody's fellow-designer at the Balloon Factory, J. W. Dunne, believed the best way of achieving stability in flight was with a V-wing, tailless configuration. With official support, he built an aircraft designated D.1, which in 1907 flew only as a glider. But his 1908 Model D.4 powered biplane, with a 20 h.p. R.E.P. engine, made a number of hops at Blair Atholl, Scotland, in July 1908, while his 1909 biplane (*above*) was so successful that he could let it fly itself while he sat back in its cockpit and wrote a report.

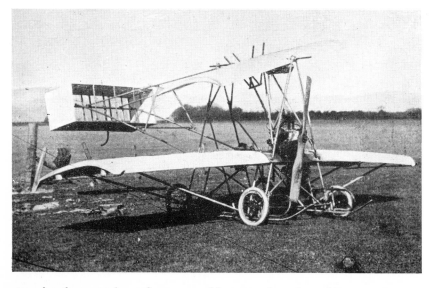

Aviators were generally regarded as either lunatics or public menaces in Britain in 1907–8; yet the foundations for our future greatness in the air were already being laid. Then, in April 1909, the War Office decided to abandon aeroplane experiments, as the cost, which totalled £2,500 by that time, was considered too great. (By comparison, Germany spent £400,000 on military aviation in 1909.) But both Cody and Dunne continued to develop their aircraft privately. Other pioneers were also at work, and the brothers Oswald, Horace and Eustace Short – official balloon-makers to the Aero Club – started to make their first aeroplane under railway arches at Battersea.

71. Another aeroplane of 1910 was this powered version of Preston Watson's design, with a 30 h.p. Humber engine.

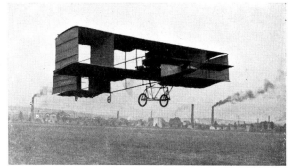

72–73. In 1907, J. T. C. Moore-Brabazon (now Lord Brabazon of Tara) built at Brooklands a Buchet-engined biplane (*above left*). It would not leave the ground; so he went to France to learn to fly, and on 4th December 1908 made a flight of 450 yards in a Voisin at Issy-les-Moulineaux (*above right*).

74. Five months later, in his own Voisin, named *Bird of Passage*, he flew nearly 500 yards at the Aero Club's new aerodrome at Leysdown in Kent. This is officially recognised as the first flight by a British pilot in Britain.

75–76. The Short brothers moved their factory from Battersea (*left*) to Leysdown in 1909, and completed a tailless biplane of their own design for Frank (later Sir Francis) McClean, whose help had enabled the Aero Club to have its own aerodrome and headquarters. This aeroplane (*right*) never flew; but, following a visit from Orville and Wilbur Wright, the Shorts began to build the Wright biplane under licence. Their first order was for six aircraft, worth £8,400.

Of all the British pioneers, there is none more worthy of honour than Sir Alliott Verdon-Roe, founder of the great Avro Company. Like many of our finest designers and airmen, he was first inspired by the birds when, as a Merchant Navy officer, he watched albatrosses soaring over his ship at sea. He then began building models and . . .

77. . . . when the *Daily Mail* organised a model-flying contest at Alexandra Palace, London, in March 1907, the young A. V. Roe won first prize. His 8-foot tail-first model flew more than 100 feet.

78. With his £75 prize Roe built a full-size version of his model at Brooklands race track in Surrey. It was the first to combine banking and 'climb-dive' controls in one column, like a modern joystick.

79. On 8th June 1908 Roe left the ground for the first time at Brooklands in his full-size aircraft, which was powered by a 24-h.p. Antoinette engine. But when a committee of the Royal Aero Club met twenty years afterwards to decide who, officially, was the first British aviator to fly in Britain they decided that Roe's hops could not be regarded as proper sustained and controlled flights.

80. Unwanted at Brooklands, Roe transferred his experiments to Lea Marshes in 1909. No longer able to afford to hire the Antoinette engine, he built a small triplane and covered its wings with brown paper, in the hope that it would be light enough to fly with a 9-h.p. J.A.P. motor. In this aircraft, on 13th July 1909, he became the first Briton to fly in an all-British aeroplane. His triplane is preserved in the National Aeronautical Collection at South Kensington.

81. July 1909. In England, as a reward for his achievements, A. V. Roe awaited prosecution as a danger to public safety. In France the stage was set for drama as two airmen prepared to take up aviation's first big challenge – the flight across 22 miles of water between Calais and Dover. One was Louis Blériot, who in October of the previous year had won fame at last with a 25½-mile cross-country flight (*above*), during which he landed three times. This time there could be no landings *en route*.

82. The other was English-born Hubert Latham, who took up the dangerous sport of flying because doctors said he had only a year to live. Latham set out first in his graceful Antoinette on 19th July; but after two miles he was forced down by engine failure.

85. Composite picture of Blériot, Mme Blériot and his Type XI monoplane, which was taken to London by rail after the Channel flight and seen by more than 120,000 people.

83. Before Latham could make a second attempt Blériot, his foot swathed in bandages following yet another accident, made an early-morning start on 25th July. Seldom more than a few feet above the sea and without a compass, he lost his bearings in mid-Channel. Then the 24-h.p. Anzani engine began to overheat. Just in time, a providential shower cooled it and . . .

84. . . . Blériot landed in a meadow behind Dover Castle. The *Daily Mail* £1,000 prize had been won.

An Industry is Born

BLÉRIOT'S achievement, more than anything else, convinced the man in the street that aviation was no longer merely the hazardous, hopeless hobby of a few cranks, but might have a future of some sort. Few realised the military significance of the first flight over Britain's moat. Still fewer expected the event to become commonplace within a decade, especially when Latham again ended up in the sea on his second attempt to fly the Channel.

But aviators ceased to be objects of derision in Britain, and the charges against A. V. Roe were dropped. Men who wanted to build or fly aeroplanes no longer felt bound to cross to France, and names that would one day be famous began to appear in our pioneer air journals, *Flight* and *The Aero*. The Short brothers were busy building Wright biplanes at Leysdown. On the seashore at Marske, near Saltburn, Robert Blackburn made a brief flight in a strange monoplane, with a garden chair for a seat and a steering-wheel to work its controls.

Earlier in the year a new company named Handley Page Ltd. had taken a stand at the Aero Show staged by the Society of Motor Manufacturers and Traders at Olympia, exhibiting an unusual collection of aircraft they had built for other designers. On 17th June they opened at Barking the first British factory constructed exclusively for the manufacture of aeroplanes, and shortly afterwards young Frederick Handley Page produced the first aeroplane of his own design.

At the start of the year only Cody, an American, could claim to have flown with any success in Britain. Even in France only nine airmen were making regular flights. In America there were, perhaps, another six or seven who had flown. But the ranks filled rapidly in 1909. First flights began to be reported from many countries, and even women began to take to the new sport.

The fair sex had, of course, played their part in the progress of flying right from the early days. Mme Blanchard was almost as famous a balloonist as her husband, and in England the Aero Club was founded as the result of a suggestion made by Miss Vera Hedges Butler during a balloon flight in 1901. It was hardly to be expected that they would leave powered flight to the menfolk, and in October 1909 aviation had its first woman 'driver'.

As far as the aircraft themselves were concerned, the Wright biplanes could still be relied on to fly farther and better than almost anything else. But the disadvantage of their catapult launching system, which tied them to their home airfields, and the fact that their design was virtually incapable of development to keep pace with new ideas and knowledge, gave them only another year of real usefulness and leadership.

French designers in particular began to develop safe and efficient aircraft, helped by the availability of an incredible new engine named the Gnome rotary, which had been invented by Monsieur Seguin and revolutionised flying for the next five years.

With so many new and promising aircraft being built it was inevitable that someone should suggest matching them against each other, and most leading

French, British and American aviators competed in the world's first flying meeting at Rheims, which was attended by a quarter of a million people. They got their money's worth of excitement, for records were broken every day.

Nobody was killed at Rheims; but Blériot had a serious accident after breaking the speed record in his new monoplane with an 80-h.p. V-8 engine – the most powerful at the meeting – and several Voisins were wrecked. This only added to the excitement, and flying meetings began to have their place in the sporting calendar all over the world.

Nor was aviation any longer merely a sport. It was not yet reliable enough to become a method of public transport, although Germany started a passenger service with Zeppelin airships in 1910. But the Zeppelin had another, more sinister application, and more and more people began to see the aeroplane too as a formidable new weapon of war.

Evolution of the first seaplanes and experiments in flying aircraft off and on to warships promised long-range reconnaissance 'eyes' for the world's battle-fleets. Aeroplanes began to sprout machine-guns and bombs. A French designer even produced an aircraft that was armoured against ground fire.

Two Bristol Boxkite biplanes took part in Army manœuvres on Salisbury Plain in September 1910, during which the first wireless messages were transmitted from an aircraft in flight to a ground station. Next month the scope of the Balloon Section of the Royal Engineers was enlarged 'to afford opportunities for aeroplaning', and in December the War Office bought for £400 an aeroplane designed by a young man named Geoffrey de Havilland.

Thinking it would be cheaper to build its own aeroplanes than to encourage private enterprise, the War Office next renamed the Balloon Factory the Army Aircraft Factory (later Royal Aircraft Factory) and decided to standardise on aircraft types produced there, much to the dismay of the embryo British aircraft industry. On 1st April 1911 the Balloon Section R.E. was replaced by the Air Battalion, and six officers were attached for duty. Exactly one month earlier one Marine and three naval officers had begun flying lessons at Eastchurch on Short biplanes loaned by Frank McClean.

By the beginning of 1912 the British Government was so alarmed by reports of activity in Germany and France that it appointed a committee to consider the whole question of military aviation. As a result of its recommendations the Royal Flying Corps came into being on 13th May 1912, with military and naval wings. After that, the privately-owned British aircraft companies did not care if the War Office standardised on Farnborough-built Henson steam carriages; because they knew that the Admiralty, under Winston Churchill, would buy the best aircraft available, wherever they were built.

Nevertheless they turned up in force for the important War Office military trials in August 1912, which were intended to give British companies a chance to prove the superiority of their designs in competition with the latest French aircraft, following criticism that most of the aircraft then in service with the R.F.C. were French-built. To the surprise of many people, Cody won convincingly with his massive 'Cathedral' and collected £5,000 in prize-money. But the R.F.C. continued to use French and 'Factory' built aircraft, and when war started in August 1914 there were few British privately-built aeroplanes among the machines the R.F.C. and R.N.A.S. took to France. Among the few, however, were the Avro 504 and Sopwith Tabloid biplanes, which set the standard for the whole succession of British military aeroplanes that followed

86–87.   One of the first Wright biplanes built in England by the Short brothers was bought by Alec Ogilvie, who made many fine flights in it from Camber Sands, near Rye, including a non-stop flight of 139¾ miles, in 3 hours 55 minutes, in 1910. These two photographs show it being prepared for flight and being retrieved afterwards from the broad sands, which made an ideal 'airfield.'

88–89.   The Short-built Wright, lacking wheels, was moved to and from its hangar on a wheeled trolley, with the aid of a windlass. Powered during its best flights by an N.E.C. engine, it retained the two chain-driven propellers of the very first Wright biplane.

90.   Some of aviation's greatest pioneers are shown in this photograph, taken at the Aero Club's headquarters at 'Mussel Manor'. Standing from left to right, are the owner of 'Mussel Manor', Oswald, Horace and Eustace Short, Frank McClean, Griffith Brewer, Frank Hedges Butler and Dr. Lockyer of the Aero Club, and Warwick Wright, another pioneer aircraft constructor. Seated are J. T. C. Moore-Brabazon, Wilbur and Orville Wright, and Charles Rolls.

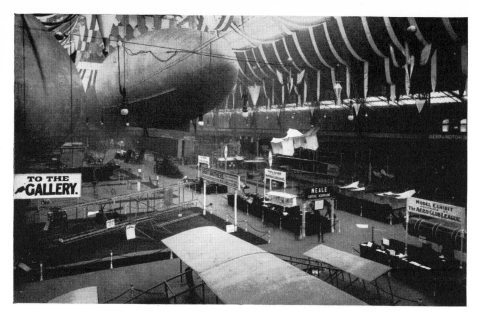

91. Following the success of the first Aero Show staged in the Grand Palais in Paris in 1908, a British Aero Show was held at Olympia in March 1909. Exhibits included Cody kites and the partially completed 'Battersea' Short No. 1; but all the really practical aeroplanes were French.

92. Engines at the Aero Show included the revolutionary Gnome rotary, which gave an honest 50 h.p. for a weight of only 165 lb. To save weight and improve cooling, its crankshaft remained still and the cylinders rotated with the propeller. Although regarded at first as a freak, it was responsible for much of the progress made in aviation for the next few years.

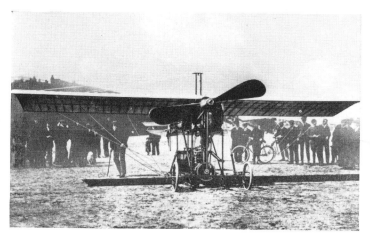

93. Robert Blackburn's monoplane left the ground at the first attempt in April 1909, but side-slipped in a turn and was wrecked. It had a 35-h.p. Green engine.

94. First Handley Page aircraft was this 20-h.p. monoplane with graceful, swept-back, crescent-shaped wings. The now-famous designer is seen at the controls.

95–96. On 8th July 1908 Mme Thérèse Peltier (*left*) became the first woman passenger in an aeroplane, by flying with Léon Delagrange at Milan. Inevitably, it was only a matter of time before a woman occupied the pilot's seat; and in October 1909 Mme la Barronne de Laroche (*right*) gained the first pilot's licence granted to a woman.

97. The pioneer Flying Meeting at Rheims in August 1909 gave the public an opportunity to see the tremendous progress made in six years of powered flight. Hubert Latham set up a world speed record by rounding the pylons in his Antoinette for 100 kilometres at 42 m.p.h. Henry Farman – flying an improved Voisin-type biplane built by himself – gained world duration and distance records; and Glenn Curtiss, piloting his *Golden Flyer*, won the new Gordon Bennett International Trophy for the fastest speed over a 20-kilometre course.

98. Latham's Antoinette.

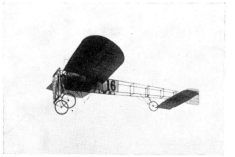

99. Delagrange's Blériot.

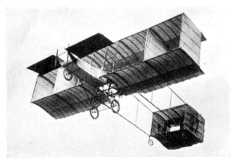

100. Bunau-Varilla's Voisin.

101. Sixty horse-power in the air; one on the ground. One of Robert Esnault-Pelterie's steel-framed, streamlined R.E.P. monoplanes being towed to the starting line at Rheims.

102. Following the success of the Rheims meeting, the first British flying meetings were held at Blackpool and Doncaster in October 1909. Sensation at Blackpool was Hubert Latham's flight in his Antoinette monoplane in a gale to avoid disappointing the crowd – the first time a pilot had ever flown deliberately in bad weather. At Doncaster, Cody (*right*) completed his naturalisation as a British subject and announced his intention of trying for the *Daily Mail* £1,000 prize offered for the first British pilot to fly a mile in an all-British aircraft.

103-4. Chief prize-winner at Blackpool was Henry Farman (*right*), who won £2,400 in a biplane of his own design. He shared the aircraft with Louis Paulhan (*above*), who made several flights in half a gale.

105. Cody had an accident at Doncaster, and before he could attempt to win the *Daily Mail* prize Moore-Brabazon completed the required circular mile in this Short No. 2, which resembled the Wright biplane but had improved controls and a 60-h.p. Green engine.

106. (*Right*) Shortly afterwards, Moore-Brabazon killed once and for all the expression 'Pigs might fly', which had been used for years by debunkers of flying, by carrying a pig in a waste-paper basket tied to the wing of his biplane.

Early leader of British aviation was Claude Grahame-White, who had organised a flying school at Pau in France in 1909 and bought land to build an aerodrome at Hendon in 1910. His duel with Louis Paulhan, in April 1910, for the Daily Mail prize of £10,000 for the first flight between London and Manchester was one of the most exciting races in aviation history. Taking off an hour after Paulhan, the British pilot made one of the first night flights in an effort to overtake him. But the Frenchman won, completing the journey in 12 hours.

107. Grahame-White with one of his first passengers.

109. Louis Paulhan.

108. Grahame-White's Farman being prepared for the race.

110. Paulhan with his Farman biplane at Lichfield, during his night stop.

111. Forty years afterwards, at the age of 67, Paulhan covered the same course in 19 minutes in a Meteor jet-fighter.

112. First Englishman to fly the Channel and first aviator to complete a two-way crossing was Charles Rolls, who made the return flight, without landing in France, in a French-built Wright on 2nd June 1910. Next month he was killed, but his name lived on in the great Rolls-Royce engineering company he had formed with Sir Henry Royce.

113. Robert Loraine, the famous actor, made the first crossing of the Irish Sea in 1910, during which the engine of his Farman stopped six times and many of its bracing wires snapped.

114. On 18th December 1910 T. O. M. Sopwith made a non-stop flight of 177 miles from Eastchurch to Beaumont, Belgium, to win the £4,000 Baron de Forest prize.

115. The first aeroplane flight over the Alps was made on 23rd September 1910, by the Peruvian pilot Georges Chavez, in a Blériot monoplane. He crashed on landing and was killed. Four months later his fellow-countryman Jean Bielovucic made a completely successful crossing.

116. Bristol Boxkites under construction. Three of them were sent on a sales tour of Australia and India, and eight were ordered by the Russian Government.

1910, *as we have seen, was a year of great flights. The aeroplane had begun to go places, and aviation was fast becoming an industry, complete with factories, aerodromes and flying schools. The first real aerodromes were at Brooklands, Hendon and the Aero Club field at East-church. Most of the 'characters' found their way to Brooklands, including one gentleman who always tried to land 6 feet too high or 6 feet too low, so that his average landing was theoretically perfect. Another newcomer made himself so unpopular that the 'regulars' bombed him out with fireworks, to which he replied with bullets from his revolver!*

117. Graham Gilmour flying his Boxkite over Henley Regatta – an escapade which led to suspension of his flying licence for one month.

118. Flying was no longer a sport for supermen. Anyone with sufficient cash and courage could learn to 'drive' an aeroplane.

119. First aeroplane built by Geoffrey de Havilland in 1910. It crashed; but he built another, which was bought by H.M. Balloon Factory and earned him a job there as draughtsman-cum-test-pilot.

120. Hendon aerodrome opened officially on 1st October 1910. Eight sheds were erected by the Blériot Company, three of which were leased to Horatio Barber's Aeronautical Syndicate Ltd., makers of the Valkyrie tail-first monoplane (Fig. 148).

121. This 'oscillator machine' was built at Brooklands to teach pilots to fly without leaving the ground. It could be made to bank, climb and dive in light winds, and was a forerunner of the £125,000 electronic flight simulators of today.

122. As well as building aeroplanes, the British and Colonial (Bristol) Company opened flying schools at Lark Hill on Salisbury Plain (*above*) and Brooklands. These schools trained more than 300 pilots by August 1914 – 80 per cent of the number available at the outbreak of war.

123. Scene at Brooklands. George Barnes' Humber-built Blériot flying over G. White's biplane.

124. All-too-frequent end of a flight at Brooklands. Cordonnier's Hanriot being extracted from the River Wey.

125. By 1910 America, France and Britain no longer had a monopoly in aviation. The first flight by a German aeroplane had been made by the Grade triplane on 12th January 1909. And one of the members of the Aerial Experiment Association – J. A. D. McCurdy – returned home to Canada with his *Silver Dart* biplane and flew it half a mile at Baddeck Bay, Nova Scotia, on 23rd February 1909. This was, officially, the first flight by a British subject in the Empire. Soon afterwards he formed the Canadian Aerodrome Company and built two more aircraft – Baddeck 1 and 2 – the first of which (*above*) was demonstrated before the Canadian Militia Council on 11–12th August 1909. Both eventually crashed and so did McCurdy's firm, but he later founded the Canadian aircraft industry by managing a subsidiary of the American Curtiss Company which built Curtiss 'Jenny' trainers at Toronto during the 1914–18 war.

126. In Switzerland, on 28th August 1910, Armand Dufaux flew 80 kilometres over the Lake of Geneva in the aircraft built by his brother Henri and himself.

127. In Russia Igor Sikorsky abandoned helicopters and flew successfully in his S-2 biplane. Another, unidentified, Russian built this strange aircraft.

128. The Belgian Vreedenburgh biplane flew in 1910, powered by a 40-h.p. Anzani engine.

129. First aircraft built by the great Dutch designer Anthony Fokker was the *Spin* (Spider) of 1911.

Despite the rise of the aeroplane and a decline in ballooning, there was still much interest in airships in 1910. Several were designed and built at H.M. Balloon Factory; the American explorer Walter Wellman made an unsuccessful attempt to cross the Atlantic in his airship the America; and the German Army spent vast sums of money developing Count von Zeppelin's great metal-framed, streamlined airships, some of which were 680 feet long. Most formidable military aircraft of their time, they were also the first air-liners. The twenty-passenger Deutschland and her successors, the Deutschland II, Schwaben, Viktoria Luise, Hansa and Sachsen carried 35,000 passengers a total of 170,000 miles between 1910 and 1914.

130. *Nulli Secundus*, British military airship No. 1, was developed by Col. Capper and S. F. Cody. It first flew in September 1907.

131. Walter Wellman.

132. A German Zeppelin of 1910 – the year in which the Zeppelin Company opened the first air passenger service between Constance and Berlin.

Many of the pioneers tried to build a successful seaplane. They thought they would hurt themselves less in a crash on to water and knew that navies would be interested in an aircraft that could act as far-ranging eyes for a battle-fleet. Curtiss fitted pontoons to his June Bug, *renamed it* Loon, *and tested it in January 1909; but it would not leave the water.*

133-4. On 28th March 1910 this incredible aircraft built by Henri Fabre made the first successful seaplane flight at Martigues, France.

135. Naval aviation owes its beginnings to Glenn Curtiss. In the autumn of 1910 he persuaded the U.S. Navy to fit a wooden platform over the deck of the U.S. cruiser *Birmingham*, and on 14th November Eugene Ely made a successful flight from this platform in a standard Curtiss biplane at Hampton Roads, Virginia. The aircraft-carrier had been born.

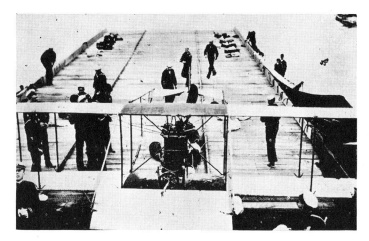

136–7. Eugene Ely completed his 'double', on 18th January 1911, by landing on the U.S.S. *Pennsylvania*. His Curtiss biplane was dragged to a halt by sandbags attached to each end of ropes stretched across the wooden flight deck so that they were picked up by hooks under the aircraft's landing gear. The arrester gear fitted to modern aircraft carriers uses exactly the same principle.

138. The first really practical seaplane was built and flown by Glenn Curtiss on 26th January 1911, and he soon became the world's outstanding expert on water-based aircraft.

139. On 17th February 1911 Curtiss paid a flying visit in his seaplane to the U.S.S. *Pennsylvania*, in San Diego Bay, and is shown here being hoisted aboard the cruiser. This flight, more than anything else, convinced the U.S. Navy that aircraft could be of use to a battle-fleet, and Curtiss was given a contract to build an amphibian.

140. This first British seaplane was built by A. V. Roe for Cdr. Oliver Schwann of the Royal Navy. He crashed it, and before it was rebuilt, and flown successfully by Major S. V. Sippe, Col. Stanley-Adams had taken off in a Lakes seaplane, based on Curtiss's design and built by A. V. Roe.

141. By now it was obvious that the aeroplane had its uses for war. Even Antoinette put aside their graceful sporting monoplanes and built this military prototype.

142. Voisin, too, had their eyes on new markets when they fitted a machine-gun to this biplane exhibited at the Paris Aero Show.

143. Another view of the military Antoinette monoplane. One of the first streamlined aircraft, it had a cantilever wing, without any external bracing, a 'spatted' four-wheel main undercarriage, and was extensively armoured for protection against ground fire. It was too heavy to fly more than a few yards, but ranks as one of the most remarkable concepts of its time.

One of the earliest commercial uses of the aeroplane was to carry mail – the first air mail service being organised in India in 1911 by Capt. (later Sir) Walter Windham. It paved the way for the famous Coronation Air Mail Service later the same year, when 100,000 letters and cards were flown between Hendon and Windsor by pilots from the Blériot and Grahame-White Schools at Hendon.

145. One of the special postcards printed for the Air Mail Service.

144. Putting the finishing touches to one of the Blériot monoplanes used to carry the Coronation mail.

146. This Blériot monoplane had 'Aerial Mail' painted under its wings.

147. Among visitors to Hendon was Winston Churchill, here seen with Lord Northcliffe.

148. The first air cargo – a box of Osram lamps – was carried by one of Horatio Barber's tail-first Valkyrie monoplanes on 4th July 1911.

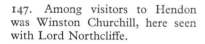

149.   First non-stop flight from London to Paris was made by Pierre Prier, chief instructor at the Blériot School, Hendon, in April 1911.

150.   A Prier monoplane from the Bristol Flying School over Stonehenge in 1912.

151.   The first twin-engined aeroplane – the Short 'Tandem Twin' of 1911, which was built for Frank McClean. As the pilot sat between the two 50-h.p. Gnome engines, it was more usually called the 'Gnome Sandwich'.

152.   Early in 1911 Henry Farman flew with five passengers. Blériot took up the challenge and lifted these six brave souls in his *Aerobus*. Then, on 23rd March, Louis Breguet carried eleven passengers for 5 kilometres; only to be beaten next day by Roger Sommer, who carried twelve.

153.   Aviation was becoming more scientific by 1912, and, following the first use of sandbags by Esnault-Pelterie to prove the wings of his 1911 R.E.P. strong enough for flight, Bristols tested the wings of their Coanda monoplane in the same way. From such humble beginnings have come the giant structure test rigs of today.

154.   The year 1912 saw the real start of military flying in Britain. The Royal Flying Corps was formed in May, with Military and Naval Wings, and a Central Flying School was set up on Salisbury Plain to train pilots for the new Service. The Admiralty had foreseen the value of aeroplanes for reconnaissance, gunnery-spotting and anti-submarine duties with the Fleet; and in January 1912 one of the original Eastchurch-trained Naval pilots, Cdr. C. R. Samson, had flown a Short biplane from a platform on H.M.S. *Africa*. The Admiralty demonstrated the possibilities of its new wing during a Review of the Fleet by H.M. King George V in May. A runway was erected on H.M.S. *Hibernia*, and . . .

155.   From this runway Cdr. Samson made the first flight from a moving ship. His Short S.27 biplane took off whilst the vessel was steaming at $10\frac{1}{2}$ knots.

156.   The S.38 was fitted with air-bags, so that it could alight on the water, if necessary. But Samson landed ashore, at Lodmoor. Soon afterwards he was appointed to command the Naval Wing of the R.F.C., which became the Royal Naval Air Service on 1st July 1914.

157–8.   Frank McClean caused a sensation on 10th August 1912 by flying his Short biplane through Tower Bridge, and then hopping and taxying under the remaining bridges to Westminster, where he alighted. Reprimanded by the police, he promised not to leave the water again until he had taxied down-river, past Tower Bridge. When he did attempt to take off, he crashed.

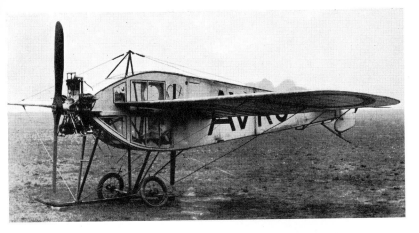

159. Formation of the R.F.C. brought fresh hope to struggling British designers like A. V. Roe, who, in April 1912, built this monoplane – the first aeroplane with an enclosed cabin to fly anywhere in the world. From it he developed a cabin biplane, which he entered for the important Military Trials staged by the War Office on Salisbury Plain. Altogether, 19 aircraft took part in the Trials, which included speed of assembly, ability to fly for three hours, rate of climb, gliding, fuel consumption, range, speed, quick take-off and rough-weather tests.

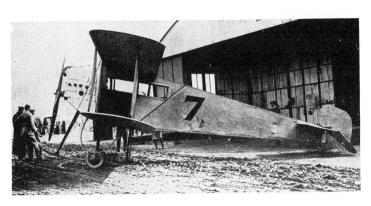

160. The Avro cabin biplane won the quick-assembly test, in 14½ min., and the fuel-consumption test. Soon after, its pilot became one of the first to survive a spin.

161. Three Deperdussin monoplanes were entered for the Military Trials, two of them built in England. One, piloted by Prevost, won the second prize of £2,000.

162–3. Other entries included the Bristol biplane (*left*) and the Bristol monoplane designed by M. Coanda (*right*).

164. Winner of the Military Trials was Cody, who collected a total of £5,000 prize money. Much of the credit belonged to the 120-h.p. Austro-Daimler engine which pushed his massive 'Cathedral' through the air fast enough to ensure victory in the speed-range test, which was judged most important of all. Whilst everybody admired Cody, most observers felt that the prizes should have gone to the Hanriot monoplane and Avro biplane.

165. Geoffrey de Havilland's B.E.2, with 70-h.p. Renault engine, was not allowed to compete in the Military Trials, having been built at the Royal Aircraft Factory. It completed some tests unofficially, and beat all comers in the speed-range and climb tests. It was the outstanding British military aeroplane of its day and, piloted by its designer, set up a British altitude record of 10,560 ft. This production-type B.E.2 was built by Vickers. Unfortunately, like the Dunne tailless aircraft, the B.E.2 was designed to have inherent stability. As a result it was not quickly manœuvrable in combat and suffered appalling casualties when used in the 1914–18 War.

166. Another superb prototype of 1912 was the Avro 500, which marked the turning point of A. V. Roe's fortunes. From it was developed the famous Avro 504, which remained in service with the R.F.C. and, later, the R.A.F. for nearly 20 years.

167. Even more sensational was the Sopwith Tabloid, demonstrated at Hendon in November 1913 by a young Australian named Harry Hawker. Carrying a pilot, passenger and fuel for $2\frac{1}{2}$ hours, it could climb to 1,200 ft. in one minute and fly at 92 m.p.h., with an 80-h.p. Gnome engine. With the B.E.2 and Avro 500, and following a series of accidents to monoplanes, the Tabloid reversed the growing preference for monoplanes, which did not return to favour for 20 years.

168. Because of its anti-rust paint, the first really successful Handley Page monoplane was known as the Yellow Peril or Antiseptic. With a top speed of 60 m.p.h., it made a famous flight over London from Barking to Brooklands, piloted by Edward Petre.

169–70. Preston Watson's 1910 aircraft (*left*), with a 30-h.p. Humber engine, was flown many times at Errol by Watson, his brother James and Archie Dickie. In 1914, his 60 h.p. Anzani-powered biplane (*right*) took part in a safety competition near Paris. Soon afterwards he was killed whilst serving with the Royal Naval Air Service.

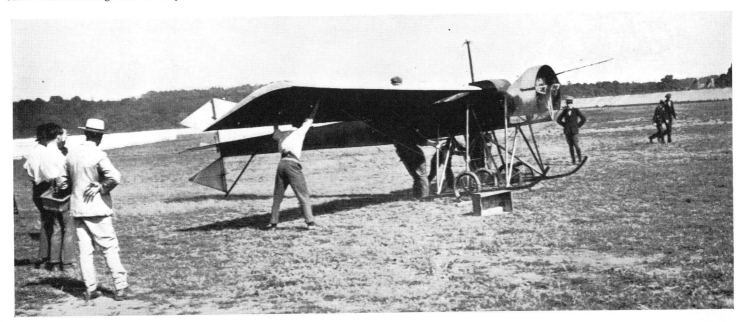

171. Second Blackburn design was the Mercury of 1911. Several were built and flown successfully. They were used by the Blackburn Flying School at Filey, and a single-seat development, built in 1912, is still flown regularly at air displays in Britain.

More Flights
of Fancy

172. One inventor was already concerned at the noise made by aeroplanes, and designed this silencer. Others thought on grander, less orthodox lines.

173. (*Above*) Edward and Henry Petre, both of whom became famous pilots, built this monoplane, with a propeller behind its tail, in 1909. It did not fly.

174. (*Right*) Another designer resurrected the tail-propeller idea in 1914, with this Ruby monoplane. More than 30 years later it was again featured on the Douglas XB-42 bomber, which flew 2,290 miles across America at a speed of 432 m.p.h. But drive-shaft problems outweighed the advantages, and tail propellers have never become popular.

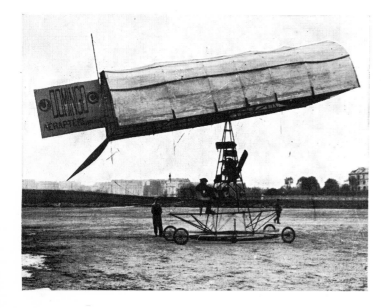

175. (*Left*) The ambitious, but quite impractical Aéraptère, designed by J. C. Domingo, was known as the 'parachute aeroplane'.

176. (*Above*) No more successful was M. Bertrand's huge monoplane, which featured a circular wing around its fuselage.

177.   Raoul Vendome, like Santos-Dumont, tried to perfect a simple, cheap aeroplane that anyone could build at home.

178.   The 12-winged 'Flying House', built by Capt. Arlington Batson in 1913, contained a sitting-room and sleeping apartments, so that its crew would be comfortable during a projected transatlantic flight.

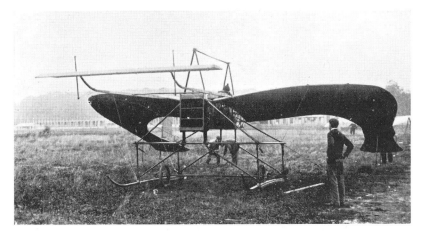

179.   The Schreick monoplane of 1910 had a horseshoe shaped wing.

180.   One of the few unorthodox types that flew successfully was the tandem wing Albessard biplane of 1914, which sported the luxury of an enclosed cabin.

181.   Best idea of all, because it was an antidote for the others, was the 'Aviator Protector' flying kit modelled by this charming young lady in 1912. Most pilots continued to prefer a leather jacket and a cap turned back to front.

182. Star attraction at Brooklands in 1913 was Adolphe Pegoud, whose aerobatic displays in a Blériot monoplane had made him the idol of Paris. The Russian pilot Nesterov was first to loop the loop; but Pegoud's repertoire included loops, tail slides, half rolls and even the difficult bunt or outside loop. He became one of the first pilots to make a parachute descent; and demonstrated a device designed to dispense with the need for smooth, clear landing fields. Only modification needed on the aircraft was the quick-release gear shown here on Pegoud's Bleriot.

183. For take-off, the aircraft was clipped onto a wire, accelerated to flying speed and released.

184. After a flight, it was simply flown under the cable until its release gear hooked on again, bringing it to a halt.

185. Recommended posture for watching Pegoud's aerobatic displays at Brooklands in September 1913.

186. An easier way of dispensing with landing fields than Pegoud's idea was to operate from water. On 10th January 1912 Glenn Curtiss followed his earlier successes by taking off in the first flying boat. It was little different from his seaplanes, except that the central float was enlarged sufficiently to accommodate the pilot and controls. Before long, Curtiss flying boats were bought by the U.S. Army and Navy, and demonstrated personally by Curtiss at Brighton, England, at the invitation of Herman Volk, son of the builder of Brighton's famous electric railway. At the controls of this Curtiss boat is Cdr. T. G. Ellyson, one of the U.S. Navy's pioneer pilots.

187. Another great name entered aviation history in August 1909, when Glenn L. Martin flew a Curtiss-type plane of his own design at Santa Ana, California. Within a few years he was in the seaplane business and one of his aircraft was used for this 'First Aerial Ferry' service across Coos Bay, Oregon.

188. Interesting British seaplane of this period was the Radley-England Waterplane, designed and flown with great success by pioneer pilot E. C. Gordon England. It had three engines, geared to drive a single propeller. Pilot and passengers sat in the twin floats. This photograph shows its first flotation tests in the River Arun, with temporary land undercarriage in position.

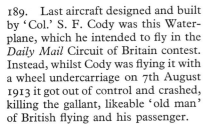

189. Last aircraft designed and built by 'Col.' S. F. Cody was this Waterplane, which he intended to fly in the *Daily Mail* Circuit of Britain contest. Instead, whilst Cody was flying it with a wheel undercarriage on 7th August 1913 it got out of control and crashed, killing the gallant, likeable 'old man' of British flying and his passenger.

190. In 1912 'Tommy' Sopwith entered the aircraft business and met with immediate success. Harry Hawker set up three altitude records in the handsome Sopwith Three-seater biplane; then won the Mortimer Singer prize of £500 with a series of flights between points on land and on water in this Sopwith Bat Boat, the first amphibian built in Europe. One Bat Boat and two Three-seaters were bought by Winston Churchill for the Naval Wing of the R.F.C.

191. (*Above*) On 15th April 1913 the first contest for the trophy presented by M. Jacques Schneider was held at Monaco. Open only to seaplanes, it consisted of a speed contest, preceded by sea-worthiness trials. Four of the seaplanes shown here took part in the event, which was won by Maurice Prévost of France in a 160-h.p. Deperdussin monoplane, at a speed of 45·75 m.p.h.

192. (*Left*) Britain took part in the Schneider Trophy contest for the first time in 1914, when Howard Pixton won at Monaco in a single-seat floatplane version of the Sopwith Tabloid, with a 100-h.p. Gnome engine. His average speed was 86·78 m.p.h. and he also set a new speed record for seaplanes of 92 m.p.h.

193-4. Ambitious project of 1912 was the Bristol X.2, with a Hydroped undercarriage designed by Sir Dennistoun Burney. This consisted of three legs carrying a series of hydrofoils and a water propeller (*right*). At rest, the X.2 floated on its boat-shaped hull. For take-off its engine first drove the water propeller. As it gathered speed, the Hydroped undercarriage was supposed to raise the hull clear of the water, until the pilot could switch to the flying propeller and take off. When towed behind a destroyer, the X.2 became airborne like a kite, before crashing.

195. Canada's first military aircraft was this 1914 Burgess-Dunne seaplane, one of several built in America to the designs of J. W. Dunne, the ex-Farnborough pioneer. Others were used by the U.S. Navy.

196. A great early contribution to air safety was this gyroscopic Automatic Pilot invented by Dr. Elmer Sperry in 1913. Its modern counterparts fly aircraft far more accurately than any human pilot.

197. One of the most spectacular events in aviation history occurred when Dr. Sperry's son Lawrence won a 50,000-franc Safety Prize at Paris in 1914. He brought this Curtiss flying boat low over the city, with his hands off the controls and his passenger standing on the wing, to prove the efficiency of its Automatic Pilot.

198–200.   After the serious pioneers and sporting pilots came, inevitably, the stunt pilots. The public wanted thrills, and men like the American Lincoln Beachey obliged. Recklessly brave, he scooped up handkerchiefs with the wing-tips of his Curtiss biplane, flew under Niagara Falls bridge and beat the racing motorist, Barney Oldfield, in this aircraft *v.* car race at Los Angeles in February 1914. He died when a monoplane of his own design folded up in the air over San Francisco Bay, during the World's Fair Exhibition of 1915.

Famous European pilot was Lt. Jean Conneau (*top right*) of the French Army, who raced as 'André Beaumont'. Flying Blériot monoplanes, he won in 1911 the Paris-Rome race, the 1,061-mile Circuit of Europe and the great Circuit of Britain race organised by the *Daily Mail*. No less popular was Gustav Hamel (*right*), who won many races, including the 1913 Aerial Derby.

201.   Grahame-White did more than anyone to make Britain air-minded in 1910–14. He toured the country in a seaplane labelled 'Wake up England'; and organised week-end races at Hendon, which attracted regular crowds of 25,000 people. Here, his biplane is shown in flight during an international air race which he won there on 25th September 1913.

202. (*Right*) The *Daily Mail* continued its efforts to popularise flying and in 1912 organised the first of the Aerial Derby races, which continued until 1923. Seven pilots set off from Hendon on the 81-mile circuit of London. The winner was Sopwith, with Hamel in second place, both flying Blériot monoplanes.

203. (*Below*) To satisfy the demand for joy-rides at Hendon, Grahame-White built the Aerobus biplane. His chief pilot, Louis Noel, used it to set up a new world load-carrying record, by flying with nine passengers for nearly 20 minutes.

204. (*Right*) A less serious load-carrying record was claimed by Louis Noel when he carried the world's heaviest passenger – a lady weighing 19 st. 12 lb.

205. Night racing and night flying of aircraft with their wings outlined by strings of electric-light bulbs were other attractions at Hendon. Richard Gates mounted a 200,000 candle-power searchlight on this Farman, and used it to signal 'England expects every man will do his duty and support aviation'.

206. Naval and military aircraft on review at Hendon, 28th September 1912. Earlier in the month two squadrons of eight aircraft had taken part in the Army's autumn manœuvres. Results were promising; but two monoplanes crashed and the Secretary of State for War banned monoplanes from the Military Wing of the R.F.C. The First Lord of the Admiralty, Winston Churchill, did not follow suit, and the spectacle of naval officers flying fast monoplanes while they plodded along in biplanes so infuriated military officers that it hastened the split between the two sections of the Service.

207–8. Despite the increase in flying activities, accidents were comparatively few, and M. Jeans Ors (*left*) and Mr. Newell (*right*) found little sale for their parachutes. Even air forces rejected them, feeling that pilots might be tempted to abandon their aircraft under fire.

209–11. Military aircraft were still unarmed; but everywhere guns and bombs were being carried experimentally. In America Lt. Riley Scott invented a primitive bombsight in 1911. In Britain a Grahame-White biplane (*above*) was demonstrated at Bisley in November 1913, with a Lewis machine-gunner seated below the pilot. Another armed Grahame-White aircraft (*right*) was displayed at the Olympia Aero Show; and the French produced a new armoured aeroplane (*below*).

212. Now that they could fly with confidence designers became ambitious. More powerful engines and the new art of streamlining produced sensational aircraft like this Deperdussin monoplane, first aircraft to fly 200 km. in an hour. Designed by Béchereau, powered by a 160-h.p. Gnome engine, and flown by Maurice Prévost, it won the Gordon-Bennett Cup in 1913 and smashed a dozen world speed records.

213. At the Royal Aircraft Factory H. P. Folland's S.E.4 scout achieved 131 m.p.h. with a 160-h.p. Gnome. Its engine was fan-cooled; the variable camber wings could be used as landing flaps; and it had a celluloid cockpit cover, single-wing struts and accurately streamlined bracing wires to reduce drag.

214. In Russia Igor Sikorsky abandoned helicopters and built the first four-motor aeroplane in 1913. Named *Le Grand*, it weighed 9,000 lb., had a span of 92 ft., and was powered by four 100-h.p. Argus engines. It made 53 successful flights before being dismantled.

215–16. Czar Nicholas II inspected *Le Grand* and was photographed with its designer (*left*) during Army manœuvres in the summer of 1913. A few months later, Sikorsky flew an improved four-motor aircraft, named *Ilia Mourometz* after a legendary Russian hero. It had a promenade deck along which passengers could walk in flight (*right*), a toilet, and a heated cabin in which meals were served. When war came, guns and bomb racks were fitted and over 70 more of these giant aircraft went into service with Russian bomber squadrons. They made 400 successful raids for the loss of only one aircraft.

217.   The first flight of *Ilia Mourometz* No. 1, in January 1914, was made with a skid undercarriage. Five months later it flew several times as a seaplane. Its wing span was 10 ft. greater than that of *Le Grand* and it weighed 10,000 lb.

218. Although smaller than the *Ilia Mourometz*, the Curtiss flying boat *America* was no less ambitious, being built for an attempted flight across the North Atlantic. Its pilot was to have been John Porte, who had been invalided out of the Royal Navy. Before it could be completed Britain was at war with Germany. Porte returned to the Navy, closely followed by the *America*, which became the forerunner of all the large Curtiss flying boats which were redesigned by Porte and flown with distinction by pilots of the Royal Naval Air Service on anti-Zeppelin and anti-U-boat patrols.

The Aeroplane goes to War

WHEN Great Britain declared war on Germany on 4th August 1914 the military aircraft was still largely a novelty.

Germany had the biggest air force, and probably the best, as many of its 260 aircraft were powered by the highly efficient Mercédès liquid-cooled engines which had enabled German pilots to set up outstanding duration and altitude records in 1914.

On the Allied side, France mustered 156 aeroplanes; while the Royal Flying Corps entered the field with 63 aeroplanes, 105 officers and 95 M.T. vehicles.

When ordered overseas, Nos. 2 and 4 Squadrons were equipped with B.E. 2's; No. 3 with Blériots and Henri Farmans; and No. 5 with Henri Farmans, Avro 504's and B.E. 8 reconnaissance aircraft.

Their pilots wrapped motor-car-tyre inner tubes round their waists as makeshift lifebelts and headed out over the Channel. They were told to ram any Zeppelins sighted – a far-from-cheering prospect, as they had no parachutes.

The Royal Naval Air Service also moved quickly into action. Its 39 landplanes, 52 seaplanes and 7 airships were, at first, concentrated at British coastal air stations; but on 1st September an expeditionary force led by Cdr. Samson was sent to Belgium.

Its pilots made the first British air raid into German territory on 22nd September. They were unsuccessful; but, on 8th October, Squadron Cdr. Spenser Grey dropped some tiny bombs on Cologne railway station; while Flt.-Lt. R. L. G. Marix attacked the Zeppelin sheds at Dusseldorf, and had the satisfaction of seeing one shed go up in flames, complete with the new and secret Zeppelin Z.IX. Both pilots were flying Tabloids.

The bomber had been born. The fighter developed more slowly, because nobody could find an efficient way of firing a machine-gun from an aircraft like the Tabloid without hitting the propeller. Then Anthony Fokker invented an interrupter gear which 'timed' the bullets so that they went between the blades; and his little monoplane fighters began driving the R.F.C. from the sky.

The D.H.2, F.E.8, F.E.2B and Vickers Gunbus helped to end the 'Fokker Scourge'; and the savage dog-fighting era started, bringing with it the first air aces – Ball, Mannock, McCudden, Bishop, von Richthofen, Boelcke, Immelmann, Guynemer and, when America entered the war, Rickenbacker and Lufbery.

So, by 1918, Tennyson's nineteenth-century vision of 'the nations' airy navies grappling in the central blue' was no longer fiction. Air power had, in fact, become such a vital part of the war machine that, on 1st April 1918, the R.F.C. and R.N.A.S. were combined in a single Service – the Royal Air Force – under the control of the newly-formed Air Ministry.

To supply the new service, the aircraft industry in Britain alone had grown from a handful of small factories, peopled with a few visionaries and craftsmen, to a vast industry, employing 350,000 men and women and producing aeroplanes at the rate of 30,000 a year – all for war. Little wonder that Orville Wright commented sadly: 'What a dream it was: what a nightmare it has become.'

219. In June 1914, the entire Military Wing of the Royal Flying Corps was concentrated at Netheravon for a month of intensive training. Its aircraft were tested under active service conditions, which seemed to prove the superiority of the B.E.2 (*right*). On 2nd July, the squadrons returned to their home stations to continue training for the autumn manœuvres. Instead, within a month, they were at war, in France.

220. (*Below*) *Royal Flying Corps in the Field*, painted by Kenneth McDonough, shows the first reconnaissance flight over enemy territory on 19th August, 1914, by Captain (now Air Chief Marshal Sir) Philip Joubert de la Ferté in a Blériot XI monoplane and Lt. Gilbert Mapplebeck in a B.E.2B. Less than a month later history was made when the first reconnaissance photographs were taken behind the enemy lines during the Battle of the Aisne.

221. Maurice Farman Shorthorn reconnaissance aircraft were used by all the Allies on the Western Front in 1914–17. These Shorthorns belonged to a Belgian squadron. Others, flown by No. 4 Squadron, R.F.C., were the first armed British aircraft used in action. They carried a Lewis machine-gun in their fuselage.

222. On 21st November 1914 three pilots of the Royal Naval Air Service, flying Avro 504's, made a successful bombing raid on the German Zeppelin works at Friedrichshaven. This is the aircraft flown by Squad.-Cdr. E. F. Briggs. His companions were Flt.-Cdr. J. T. Babington and Flt.-Lt. S. V. Sippe, a famous pre-war racing and test pilot.

223. First real fighter-scouts were Morane-Saulnier monoplanes and Sopwith Tabloids, fitted with machine-guns, which fired through their propeller arc. Metal plates on the propellers deflected bullets that would otherwise have damaged the blades. Invented by the French pilot Roland Garros, the idea was copied and improved by Anthony Fokker, who designed proper interrupter gear. This 'timed' the bullets to pass between the blades.

224. Realising the value of heavy bombing right from the start, Admiral Sir Murray Sueter asked Handley Page Ltd. for a 'bloody paralyser' for the R.N.A.S. in December 1914. The result was this H.P. o/100, which flew on 18th December 1915, and was developed into the highly successful H.P. o/400, powered by two Rolls-Royce Eagle engines.

225. Germany's powerful Mercédès water-cooled engines gave her warplanes a higher performance than most Allied aircraft in 1914–15. This L.V.G. C–1 reconnaissance biplane had a 130-h.p. Mercédés and speed of 97 m.p.h.

226. Nearly all British squadrons in France had one or two Bristol Scouts on their strength in 1915. Their armament usually consisted of the pilot's personal revolver.

227. The R.N.A.S. made extensive use of non-rigid airships (blimps) for anti-submarine patrol and convoy escort duties. About 150 of these S.S. (sea-scout) airships were built, each powered by a 75-h.p. Rolls-Royce engine and carrying a crew of three. They could fly for 17 hours at 45 m.p.h. Larger types were the C (Coastal) and the N.S. (North Sea) airships.

228. Most formidable fighter of 1915 was Anthony Fokker's Eindekker II, with a 100-h.p. Oberursel rotary engine. Armed with a machine-gun which fired through its propeller arc, it almost drove the slow and poorly armed Allied aircraft from the air, and was followed by the more powerful E.III, with two guns.

229. First aeroplane designed for air fighting was the Vickers Gunbus, the prototype of which flew before the war. It had a 'pusher' propeller, to avoid the problem of firing its gun between the propeller blades. With other 'pusher' fighters it provided the R.F.C.'s answer to the Fokker monoplane.

230. Two versions of the Voisin biplane were used extensively by the French in 1915–17. The *Avion Canon* carried a 37- or 47-mm. gun in its nose and was used to attack ground targets. The *Avion de Bombardement* was a highly-successful bomber. Both carried their fuel in streamlined tanks between the wings.

231-2. Parachutes were issued to few German pilots and to no British pilots during the 1914–18 War – a decision which cost many lives when aircraft were set on fire during dog-fights. This Guardian Angel parachute, tested from Tower Bridge, London, was used by the crews of observation balloons, which were a favourite target for fighter pilots.

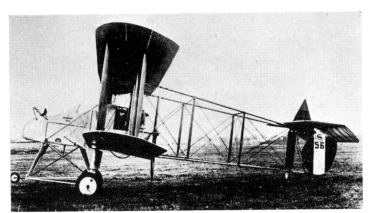

233-5. Three successful fighters of 1916–17 were the F.E.2B (*above, left*), Nieuport Scout (*above right*) and Sopwith 1½-Strutter (*right*). Both Capt. Albert Ball (43 victories) and Col. Billy Bishop (72 victories) scored many successes flying Nieuports. Those illustrated were flown by No. 1 Squadron, R.F.C. The 1½-Strutter was the first fighter to carry a rear-gunner.

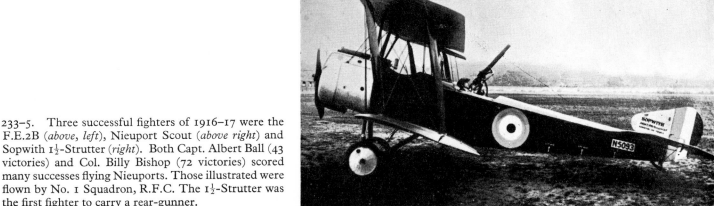

236.   No. 3 Squadron of the R.F.C., equipped with Morane parasol monoplanes, specialised in the new technique of observing and helping to correct the fire of Allied artillery.

237.   The R.F.C. and R.N.A.S. were fighting on every battle-front by 1915. This Martinsyde Scout was one of the aircraft of No. 30 Squadron which flew reconnaissance missions over the Turkish lines before the battle of Ctesiphon, in Mesopotamia.

238.   The first guided missile. This little radio-controlled monoplane was built at the Royal Aircraft Factory in 1916, to the designs of H. P. Folland and Prof. A. M. Low. To conceal its real role of flying bomb, it was known as the Aerial Target.

239.   American counterpart to the Aerial Target was the Aerial Torpedo. Designed by Dr. Elmer Sperry for the U.S. Navy, it was tested successfully at a secret flying field on Long Island in December 1917.

240. Air-to-air rockets were used with some success in the 1914–18 War. Designed by a French naval officer for destroying kite balloons or airships, these Le Prieur rockets were mounted on the interplane struts and fired electrically. Their best range was under 400 ft.

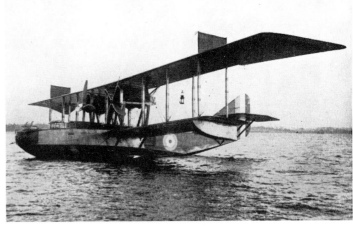

241. Over the sea, as over land, air power grew rapidly in importance. Seaplanes and airships escorted convoys and located targets for submarines and warships. Here a German Friedrichshafen FF.33h seaplane delivers despatches to U.35 in the Mediterranean.

242. Long-range flying boats like this Porte-Curtiss F.2A America patrolled the waters around Britain, helping to check the U-boat menace and even shooting down Zeppelins L.22, L.43 and L.62.

243. First successful torpedo-planes were Short seaplanes of the R.N.A.S. On 12th August 1915 a Short 184 from the seaplane carrier *Ben-My-Chree*, piloted by Flt.-Cdr. C. H. K. Edmonds, sank a 5,000-ton Turkish ship. Later came the more powerful Short 320, seen here dropping its 18-inch torpedo.

244. Seaplanes were usually lowered on to the water for take-off; but sometimes wheeled trolleys were put under their floats so that they could take off from the deck of the first primitive aircraft carriers. A variation was the skid undercarriage, with deck 'railway' to keep the aircraft straight.

245. Typical of the giant Zeppelins which bombarded Britain and menaced the Navy throughout the 1914–18 War was L.32. It made four raids before being shot down by Second Lieut. F. Sowrey of No. 39 Squadron, R.F.C., flying a B.E.2C. Of 62 operational German Zeppelins, 19 were shot down, 11 wrecked by bad weather, and 11 destroyed by accident or bombing in their sheds. The L.30 class were about 643 feet long, with a capacity of 1,907,000 cubic feet, and were powered by six 240-h.p. engines. Maximum speed was 60 m.p.h., carrying a 22-ton load. They carried incendiary and high-explosive bombs from 110 to 660 lb. in weight.

Development of Carriers

246. To make up for a shortage of aircraft carriers, single- and two-seat fighters were flown from platforms erected on the gun-turrets of warships, to protect the Fleet. This Sopwith 1½-Strutter is flying from the cruiser H.M.S. *Australia*.

247-8. Another idea was to fly a Sopwith Camel fighter from a lighter towed behind a fast destroyer. Within an hour of making this successful take-off on 11th August 1918 Lt. S. D. Culley shot down Zeppelin L.53 in flames off Ameland.

249. Although they could take off from aircraft carriers, R.N.A.S. aeroplanes still had to alight on the sea and be hoisted aboard after each flight. On 2nd August 1917 Squad.-Cdr. E. H. Dunning flew around the funnel of the newly commissioned H.M.S. *Furious* and landed his Sopwith Pup on its foredeck. In a further attempt, five days later, he was drowned: but his exploit had proved carrier landings possible, and rear landing-on decks were fitted on H.M.S. *Argus* and *Furious*.

and of the Bomber

250. By 1917 the aeroplane had become a formidable weapon of attack. One of the most impressive bombers was this three-engined Italian Caproni CA.41 triplane, which was flown by both Italian and British pilots in the last year of the war. Its wings spanned 130 feet.

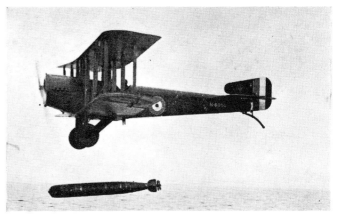

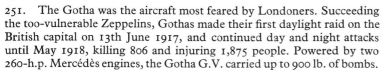

251. The Gotha was the aircraft most feared by Londoners. Succeeding the too-vulnerable Zeppelins, Gothas made their first daylight raid on the British capital on 13th June 1917, and continued day and night attacks until May 1918, killing 806 and injuring 1,875 people. Powered by two 260-h.p. Mercédès engines, the Gotha G.V. carried up to 900 lb. of bombs.

252. The Sopwith Cuckoo was the first proper carrier-based torpedo-plane, and was designed for an attack on the German Fleet in harbour in 1918. The war ended before the raid could be mounted. The aircraft's name reflected the hope that it would be able to lay its "eggs" in other peoples' nests!

253. The finest day bomber was the D.H.4, of which 1,170 were in service with the R.A.F. in 1918. Others were built in America. Here a D.H.4 of No. 27 Squadron is being bombed up at Serny Aerodrome, France. A Nieuport Scout waits to escort the bomber, which was itself able to outpace most German fighters.

254. Diving, twisting, turning, its rear gunner blazing away with his Lewis machine-gun, a D.H.9 day bomber tries desperately to shake off a flight of German Albatros D.III fighters. The finest painting cannot capture all the speed, excitement and terror of such a dog-fight. There was a chivalry among fighter pilots, which often saved an enemy whose ammunition was exhausted. But mercy was seldom shown to the crews of bombing and reconnaissance aircraft.

255-6. Germany's Red Knight – the almost legendary Baron Manfred von Richthofen, who was credited with the destruction of 80 Allied aircraft. His 'circus' of brightly-painted fighters is shown (*right*) in a photograph found on the body of a German pilot. By banding together its best pilots into single units Germany attained many successes.

257. Fokker Dr. I triplanes being pushed back to their hangers after a patrol. It was whilst flying one of these highly manœuvrable fighters that von Richthofen was shot down and killed on 21st April 1918. His successor was a young man named Hermann Goering.

258. Sopwith Camels of No. 45 Squadron, R.F.C., on Fossilienga Aerodrome, Italy. Greatest fighters of the 1914–18 War, Camels destroyed 1,281 enemy aircraft in combat.

259. Second only to the Camel was the S.E.5, designed at the Royal Aircraft Factory by H. P. Folland. These S.E.5A's equipped No. 85 Squadron, R.A.F., in France in June 1918. Like the Camel, they were armed with two machine-guns.

260–1. Both powered by 160 h.p. Mercédès engines, the Pfalz D.IIIA (*left*), and Fokker D.VII (*right*), were two of the outstanding German fighters of 1918. The Pfalz had a speed of only 103 m.p.h., but was very sturdy. The Fokker was 20 m.p.h. faster; but it was its rapid climb and lightning recovery from a dive which won the Germans 565 air combat victories over the Western Front in August 1918.

262. First armoured German aeroplane, the Junkers J.IV ground-attack and observation machine was covered with 5-mm. steel plating. Altogether 227 were built.

263. Designed for ground attack 'contour fighting', the two-seat Halberstadt CL.II was first used to hurl small bombs and hand grenades at advancing British troops in September 1917.

264. To meet and beat the best the Germans could put into the air, Britain's aircraft industry was producing warplanes at the rate of nearly 30,000 a year in 1918. This view of the Ham, Surrey, works of the Sopwith Company, shows Camel fighters under construction.

265. Women's fingers no longer merely sewed the fabric on wings and fuselages. In ever-growing numbers, they took over the saws, spanners and paintbrushes of men called up to fight.

266. Help came from across the Atlantic in 1918. American volunteer pilots had fought for years under French Command in the *Lafayette Escadrille*. Now America was in the war and these SPAD XIII fighters helped to equip the first all-American squadrons.

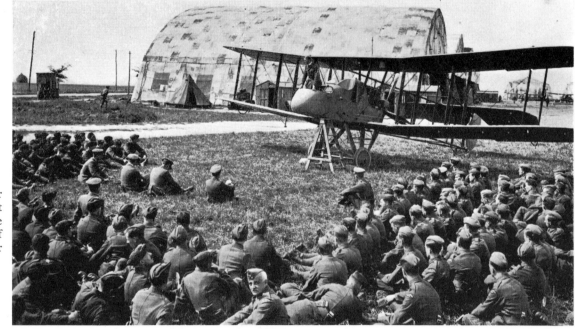

267. Spiritual aid was never overlooked, and few thought it incongruous that the padre should choose the cockpit of an F.E.2B night bomber for his pulpit.

268. Proud day for No. 4 Squadron, R.F.C., was 6th July 1917, when their aerodrome near Cassel was visited by King George V, H.R.H. the Prince of Wales and General Trenchard. Here they inspect an aircraft that crash-landed after fighting off two enemy scouts.

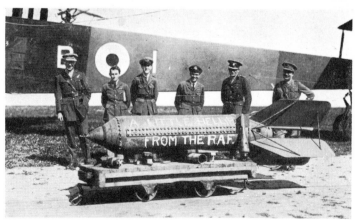

269. A few months later Trenchard formed a special unit known as the 41st Wing, with the sole duty of bombing Germany. In June 1918 this wing grew into the Independent Air Force, which dropped 550 tons of bombs on Germany in the last five months of war. The bombs shown above were the largest and smallest used.

270. Known usually as 'Harry Tates', the R.F.C.'s R.E.8 reconnaissance aircraft played a vital part in the land battles of the last two years of war, by reporting every movement of the enemy. Over 2,000 were used on the Western Front alone and they must have accumulated more flying hours than any other single type.

271. Typical of the fine aircraft with which the R.A.F. ended the war was the famous Bristol Fighter. After a disastrous start, when only two of a flight of five 'Brisfits' returned from their first action, this sturdy two-seater proved itself more than a match for the best German single-seaters, and remained in service ten years after the war ended.

272. (*Above*) Largest British aircraft used in action by the R.F.C. and R.A.F. was the twin-engined Handley Page 0/400, which set the pattern for heavy-bomber design for many years. A four-engined development, known as the Handley Page V/1500, was in service and preparing to bomb Berlin non-stop from bases in Eastern England at the time of the Armistice.

273. May 1919 – The 'war to end wars' had been won, and Handley Page 0/400 bombers of No. 48 Squadron, R.A.F., were able to fly in peace over the River Rhine at Bonn. Other 0/400s of Nos. 1 and 2 (Communications) Squadrons were already paving the way for civil airlines by providing a London–Paris transport service for delegates to the Peace Conference.

The Age of Great Flights

To meet the demands of war, aviation had grown into a tremendous industry by 1918. The aeroplane had found a purpose in life. Pilots in swift, heavily armed fighters shot each other out of the sky over the Western Front; reconnaissance 'planes reported and photographed every movement of the unhappy armies on the ground; bombers showered high-explosive and incendiary bombs on battlefield and town alike; the first dive-bombers had been built to harass further the infantryman in his muddy trench; torpedo-planes had scored their first victories against ships at sea; frail seaplanes had, to a large extent, given way to carrier-based fighters and bombers; and long-range flying-boats had helped to check the menace of the U-boat around Britain.

Almost overnight, when the Armistice was signed, the whole picture changed. The warplanes were grounded; pilots were no longer needed to fly them; the thriving industry found itself without a single order on its books.

The suddenness and completeness of the cancellation of military contracts were devastating. Some of the greatest pioneer companies were soon forced to shut up shop; others struggled on with paper plans for a new generation of private sporting aircraft and air liners for the boom in civil flying that never materialised.

The public were not ready to fly; and who could blame them? The ability of aeroplanes to kill and destroy is no yardstick by which to measure their safety or suitability for airline service. A dashing fighter 'ace' may not be the ideal pilot to inspire confidence in a nervous passenger.

In short, the public had to be convinced that the experience gained in designing, building and operating fleets of warplanes would underwrite their safety and comfort in a journey by air from A to B, and back.

Key to eventual success was that Handley Page, Bristol, Vickers and de Havilland in Britain, and Farman in France, had developed bombers big enough and sturdy enough for conversion to passenger-carrying. In parallel, Rolls-Royce, Napier, Salmson and Hispano had perfected powerful new engines that offered unprecedented standards of reliability and performance.

Civil flying was not permitted in Britain until 1st May 1919; but the Air Ministry did not waste the intervening months. In December 1918 it formed the 86th (Communication) Wing to provide a rapid means of transport to Paris for members of H.M. Government attending the Peace Conference. The service was opened next month, and by March 1919 the D.H.4's and Handley Pages of No. 1 (Communication) Squadron, based at Kenley near London, and No. 2 Squadron, based at Buc, near Paris, were operating as a busy private airline. When the service ended six months later they had made a total of 749 flights between London and Paris, with an average flight time of 2½ hours; and had carried 934 passengers, 1,008 bags of mail and 46 despatches.

From March until August an air-mail service was operated between Folkestone and Cologne by three R.A.F. squadrons, for communication with the Army of Occupation. But the Air Ministry had its work cut out to meet its military commitments. In a few months it had been depleted from 263 squadrons and 15 flights to a mere 33 squadrons. With these it had to provide a home defence force, support for the Army of Occupation, military aid for the White Russians, units to combat warlike tribes on the N.W. Frontier of India, and permanent squadrons at other key points in the Middle East. Later it was made entirely responsible for maintaining the peace in Iraq, where a few Bristol Fighters, D.H.9A's, Snipes and troop-carrying Vernons replaced many thousands of troops.

Little wonder that the Air Ministry was glad to leave airline passenger- and mail-carrying to civil operators, whilst retaining an overall control through its newly established Department of Civil Aviation.

The French Farman Company had jumped the gun on 8th February 1919 by flying about a dozen military passengers from Toussus-le-Noble airfield, near Paris, to Kenley in a converted Goliath bomber. They travelled in remarkable comfort, and were even able to eat lunch and drink champagne on the way.

Alas, it was seldom like that on the early airlines. When Air Transport and Travel Ltd. started the first daily air service between London and Paris on 25th August, passengers found things much more rugged. Their aircraft too were converted bombers; but this time they were small ones, with two or three wicker seats crammed in the fuselage where the rear gunner had once been.

To fly was an adventure to talk about for weeks. It was expensive – the London-Paris fare was £15 15s. each way – and exceedingly uncomfortable. The passengers, bunched up in woollies and leather coats and wearing helmets and goggles, were clamped into a space so small that there was no room to stand or move. There, through draughts, noise, buffeting and well-founded apprehensions, they could only sit and think how wonderful it was!

Despite the inconveniences, people did fly, and by September Handley Page Transport Ltd. were also operating regular services on the London–Paris and London–Brussels routes. Next month, the shipowners S. Instone and Company began a private airline linking Cardiff and Paris, via London, and eventually built it up into a considerable public transport service. A fourth operator, the British Marine Air Navigation Company, ran an intermittent service from Southampton to the Channel Islands and St. Malo, with flying boats.

A.T. and T. dropped out of the picture after a time; but in 1922 a newcomer, Daimler Airways, began operations. The four companies struggled on, giving valuable support to the British aircraft industry by ordering proper air liners like the Handley Page W.8B, Supermarine Sea Eagle amphibian, and the D.H.16 and 34, which helped to establish the newly formed de Havilland Company in the manufacturing business. But there was little profit in it; and everyone breathed a sigh of relief when the Government came to their aid and, on 1st April 1924, combined the four pioneer companies into a single officially backed airline named Imperial Airways.

Much the same thing had happened in France, where the pioneer Compagnie des Messageries Aériennes, Compagnie des Grands Express Aériens and Compagnie Aéronavale had combined in January 1923 to form Air Union which, 10 years later, was united with other companies to form Air France.

In every country except the United States great national airlines began to appear, usually under private ownership, but with strong Government support.

Unfortunately, airlines cannot say simply 'we are going to open a new service tomorrow from Paris to Timbuctoo'. Routes have to be surveyed, airfields levelled and stocked with fuel and supplies, and essential passenger services provided. When civil operations began in 1919, no aeroplane had flown over most of the proposed new routes.

So began the era of great flights, which continued for a decade to open up the world to air travel and inspire confidence and admiration in the still-reluctant public.

The first route to be conquered was the most difficult and dangerous of all – the North Atlantic. It was providential that the Porte-Curtiss *America* of 1914 should have been prevented from making the attempt; for even the more sturdy and powerful Curtiss NC–4, which became the first aircraft to cross the ocean in 1919, had no easy trip. Its flight, via the Azores, took 11 days, and was completely overshadowed a month later by the first non-stop flight from Newfoundland to Ireland by Captain John Alcock and Lt. A. Whitten Brown, in a converted Vimy bomber. Many other magnificent flights followed.

Particularly valuable to the development of civil flying were the series of long-distance flights made in the 1920's by pilots of the Royal Air Force, and by Sir Alan Cobham. After serving in the R.F.C., Cobham had first become a charter pilot and then joined de Havilland's. In 1921 he began his long-distance flights with a 5,000-mile circuit of Europe, and gradually became more and more ambitious until, in 1926, he flew from London to Cape Town and back, and to Australia and back, in a D.H.50. Then, in 1927, he flew 23,000 miles round Africa in a Short Singapore flying boat.

Following in his footsteps came the great Australian, Sir Charles Kingsford Smith, who, in 1928, completed the global network of British pioneering by making a 7,000-mile flight across the Pacific, from California to Brisbane, in the tri-motor Fokker *Southern Cross*, and then linked Australia and New Zealand by air for the first time, across the storm-swept, 1,400-mile Tasman Sea.

These epic flights laid the groundwork for the air routes of the world. Those by Byrd, Balchen, Amundsen and Ellsworth, over the North and South Poles, are only bearing fruit today, when airlines are beginning to save hours of journey time by flying 'great circle routes' over these desolate wastes of ice.

In parallel with the development of commercial aviation, private flying began to grow – at first slowly, and then with sudden tremendous new enthusiasm when de Havilland's produced their Moth biplane. Costing only £595, it could be flown by almost anyone, towed behind a car and kept in a garage. It made possible the flying-club movement, which spread like magic throughout the world, and led to expansion of the British aircraft industry into the Empire.

Factories to assemble Moths were set up in Australia, Canada, India, South Africa, Rhodesia and New Zealand; and the little aircraft bred a new generation of sporting pilots who achieved incredible feats of flying on less than 100 h.p.

Progress in military aviation was less spectacular, for Governments were not disposed to spend vast sums of money on new fighters and bombers when the danger of war seemed remote and finances were low. More powerful engines and a changeover to all-metal construction in the mid-'twenties improved performance. Devices like the Handley Page slot reduced accidents; but the fighters of 1930 were still biplanes with two guns, and the bombers looked little better than those of 1918.

Nevertheless, great changes were on the way. International races, like the Schneider Trophy contests, had left little doubt of the superiority of streamlined monoplane design, and the days of the biplane were numbered.

274–5. In Britain, France, Germany, Italy and America, the vast aircraft factories bred by the war suddenly became silent in November 1918. Everywhere designers began to plan civil air liners and sports-planes; but there were few customers. A handful of warplanes were converted for civil use. Some companies left the aircraft business; others turned to producing anything and everything from motor cycles to saucepans. In the Short Brothers' factory at Rochester girls still worked on Porte-Curtiss flying boats ordered for the Royal Air Force; but there was little prospect of new military contracts to follow.

276. Some units of the R.A.F. were still at war. These Fairey IIIC's and a flight of Short seaplanes were part of the North Russian Expeditionary Force at Murmansk in June 1919. They were withdrawn later in the year; but Sopwith Camels of No. 47 Squadron fought on in support of White Russian forces in South Russia until the middle of 1920.

277. Although unable to afford new equipment, air forces did not halt development and research in the post-war years. In America, Britain and France much effort was put into experiments with engine supercharging, to improve performance at height. This SPAD XIII had an exhaust-driven supercharger mounted vertically behind its cockpit. But this early development was hampered by lack of suitable alloys for the supercharger rotors.

278–9. Despite unsuccessful trials during the war, it was thought in 1919 that airships might have a future as flying aircraft carriers. This Sopwith Camel was released from H.M. airship R.33 and landed successfully by Lt. R. E. Keys of No. 212 Squadron. Further experiments were made in both Britain and America in the mid-twenties, during which fighters were released and retrieved in flight. Soon afterwards a series of disasters led to the abandoning of large military rigid airships.

280. This Camel was used in tests at the Isle of Grain to reduce the danger and damage resulting from 'ditching' at sea.

281. Air bags were developed to enable carrier-based aircraft with wheel undercarriage to alight on the water and float until help arrived.

282. Primitive deck-landing arrester gear fitted to H.M.S. *Furious* included parallel fore-and-aft cables which engaged with the aircraft's skids, and crash barriers.

283. Monstrosity of 1919 was the huge six-engined Tarrant Tabor transport tested at the renamed Royal Aircraft Establishment, Farnborough. Weighing 45,000 lb., it was intended to have a cruising range of 1,200 miles. On its first test, the top pair of its six 450 h.p. Lion engines were opened up during take-off, which caused it to tip over on its nose. After that it was abandoned.

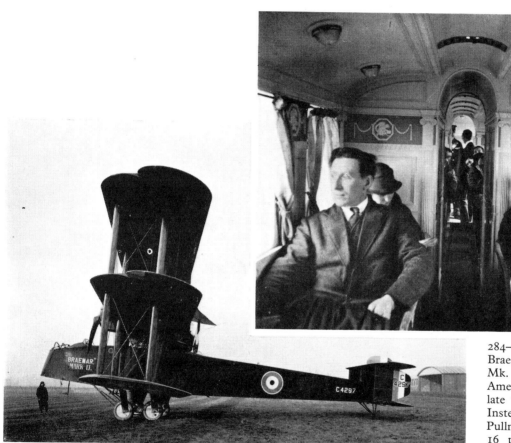

284–5. More practical was the Bristol Braemar, designed to bomb Berlin. The Mk. II version (*left*), powered by four American 400-h.p. Liberty engines, was too late to play any part in the 1914–18 War. Instead Braemar components were used in the Pullman air liner (*above*), which could carry 16 passengers in a comfortably-furnished cabin and had a top speed of 135 m.p.h.

286. Anticipating a boom in private flying, Sopwith's transformed their Pup fighter into the dainty little Dove lightplane. The boom did not materialise and Sopwith's went into liquidation. Later, they re-emerged as the now-famous Hawker company.

287. Royal leadership was given by H.R.H. Prince Albert (later King George VI), who learned to fly with the Royal Air Force at Croydon on this Avro 504K trainer. His brother, the Prince of Wales (now Duke of Windsor), was also a keen airman, as was the King of the Belgians.

The public were not air minded. Anthony Fokker knew why when he said, 'Flying will be here to stay only when it ceases to be an adventure.' In 1919, flying was 98 per cent adventure. Ex-military pilots invested their savings in war-surplus aeroplanes and 'barn-stormed' across the world giving one-man air displays and joyrides. In America the Post Office operated an air mail service from Chicago, over the Alleghenies to New York in old D.H.4's, at a cost of 30 of the original 40 flying postmen. Other pilots decided that the only way to prove the reliability and capabilities of the aeroplane was by pioneering the future air routes of the world. Greatest challenge was the North Atlantic.

288. By 24th April 1919 nine pilots had announced their intention of competing for the £10,000 *Daily Mail* prize for the first non-stop Atlantic flight. Best-known was Harry Hawker, seen here with his navigator, Lt.-Cmdr. K. Mackenzie-Grieve. Their Sopwith transport had a dinghy built into the top of its fuselage.

289. Second British team were Capt. John Alcock and Lt. Arthur Whitten-Brown, who planned, like Hawker, to attempt the west-to-east crossing from Newfoundland to the British Isles. Their aircraft was a Vickers Vimy bomber, with two 350-h.p. Rolls-Royce Eagle engines.

290. Before the British teams were ready, three Curtiss flying boats of the U.S. Navy took off from Newfoundland on 16th May 1919. Only NC–4, captained by Lt.-Cmdr. Read, completed the crossing to Lisbon, via the Azores, in 25 hours' flying time.

291. Hawker and Grieve took off in the single-engined Sopwith Atlantic two days after the Curtiss flying boats. Radiator trouble forced them down after 1,000 miles and they were mourned as dead for a week, because the steamer which rescued them had no radio.

292. At 4.15 p.m. on 14th June Alcock's grossly overloaded Vimy lumbered off the ground at St. Johns, Newfoundland, and headed out over the storm-swept Atlantic.

293. Lashed by storms, it flew on through the night. Once Alcock lost control when the big aircraft became covered with ice. It turned almost on its back, 50 feet above the waves, and only Alcock's superb flying prevented a crash.

294. Sixteen hours after take-off the Vimy landed in a bog at Clifden in Ireland and almost overturned. The Atlantic had been conquered non-stop for the first time, and the *Daily Mail* prize was won. Both Alcock and Brown were knighted by King George V.

295.   The Atlantic was flown twice more in 1919, by the British airship R.34, commanded by Major G. H. Scott, with a crew of 31 and one stowaway. Time for the outward journey from E. Fortune, Scotland, to New York was 108 hours 12 minutes. Return flight to Pulham in Norfolk took 75 hours 3 minutes. Not until five years later was the North Atlantic again crossed by air.

296.   Second £10,000 prize won by a Vimy in 1919 was for the first flight from Great Britain to Australia. Piloted by Capt. Ross Smith and Lt. Keith Smith, and with two mechanics, the bomber took 28 days for the 11,294-mile journey, from Hounslow to Port Darwin, laying the foundation for the great Empire Air Routes of the future. Ross and Keith Smith were knighted for their achievement.

297. One of the four-motor Handley Page V/1500 bombers, built to bomb Berlin from bases in Eastern England, was entered for the transatlantic contest. After Alcock and Brown's success, it went instead to America, where it was demonstrated by Major H. G. Brackley, who later became one of the leaders of British civil aviation.

298. On 13th November 1919 the V/1500 took on 1,000 lb. of American Railway Express freight for an attempted non-stop flight from New York to Chicago. Engine trouble forced it down; but American business was impressed by the possibilities of air freighting.

299. First international air-mail flight was made from Victoria, BC to Seattle on 3rd March 1919 by Eddie Hubbard and Bill Boeing, founder of the great Boeing Airplane Company. A pouch of 60 letters was carried in this C–700 seaplane – a commercial version of the 50 two-seat seaplane trainers built by Boeing for the U.S. Navy in the previous year.

300. Hero of the first coast-to-coast U.S. Air Mail flight, on 22nd February 1921, was Jack Knight, whose courage in flying on through the night, over unfamiliar country, persuaded Congress to continue the service and to light the airways with beacons.

301. First Paris–London airline service was flown by a converted Farman Goliath bomber on 8th February 1919. Passengers were military officers, as civil flying was not yet permitted in Britain.

302–3. Regular London–Paris passenger services started on 25th August 1919. Air Transport and Travel Ltd. operated converted D.H. single-engined bombers from Hounslow aerodrome (*left*). Handley Page Transport Ltd. flew converted 0/400 and V/1500 heavy bombers from Cricklewood. Enthusiasm was more evident than comfort. Passengers who travelled on A.T. and T.'s *Paris Air Special* (*right*) were well wrapped up before being stuffed into the small, uncomfortable cabin.

304–5. The D.H.9 operated by A.T. and T. (*left*) lacked even the usual plastic hood to protect its passengers from the slipstream. Despite discomforts the representative of *The Sphere* magazine (*right*) contrived to write his report en route in one of the cabin machines.

306.   Most enterprising of the pioneer British airlines was Daimler Airways Ltd., which introduced new standards of passenger service and efficient maintenance. It began operations to Paris and Brussels in 1922, later switching to Amsterdam and Cologne when the airlines agreed to disperse services to avoid harmful competition for all-too-sparse traffic.

307-8.   Daimler's D.H.34 transports offered plenty of space for passengers' luggage. First-class cabin service was also provided, and Steward Sanderson (*right*) was the first person ever employed by an airline to serve refreshments during flight.

309–10.   To ensure efficient maintenance and speedy turn-round, Daimler planned their workshops on modern lines. Engines were mounted for servicing on special trolleys which ran on a 'railway' track between the workshops and hangar.

311–12.   To speed help to aircraft stranded overseas, Daimler adapted their air liners to carry spare engines. As the engines were too long to fit into the cabin, they simply cut a hole in the fabric, through which the propeller shaft projected. The idea has been revived by one present-day airline which carries spare propellers aboard its aircraft, with the propeller tips projecting through slots in the cabin walls.

313.   Secretary of State for Air Sir Samuel Hoare and Lady Maude Hoare sampled the comfort of a Daimler Airways Special in July 1923, when they flew to Gothenberg, Sweden, for an International Aero Show. But airline pilots still sat in open cockpits, as it was considered essential to give them an all-round view unobstructed by cabin walls.

314. Early flying-boat operator was British Marine Air Navigation Company. One of its small four-seat Supermarine Channel 'boats is seen here over the Royal Pier, Southampton, in August 1919, when the city was inaugurated as the world's first Air Port.

315. First international port-to-port cross-channel air service was operated by British Marine Air Navigation Company between Southampton and Le Havre. Channel 'boats also pioneered passenger, mail and air survey flying in Fiji, Norway, New Zealand and Japan.

316. In search of new business, British Marine sent one of their aircraft on a tour of Isle of Wight seaside resorts.

317. In 1923 the Channel 'boats were replaced by three bigger, more comfortable Supermarine Sea Eagle amphibians, each able to carry six passengers in its enclosed cabin. They remained in service between Southampton and Guernsey until 1928, even though British Marine Air Navigation were merged with the three other British private airlines to form Imperial Airways Ltd. on 1st April 1924.

318. Flying boats were chosen to equip some of the early overseas airlines, including the pioneer Swiss company which began operations from Zürich in December 1919 with Italian Macchi and Savoia 'boats.

319. Oldest airline service still operated by the original company is the London-Amsterdam service of K.L.M. Royal Dutch Airlines. Passengers on the first flight, 17th May 1920, were welcomed by Dr. Albert Plesman (*right*), head of K.L.M. from its formation until his death in 1953.

320. First air service in the Belgian Congo was operated on 1st July 1920 with this flying boat. Three years later the Société Nationale pour l'Etude des Transport Aeriens (SNETA) created the Belgian national airline, SABENA, to open up Congo air routes in addition to European services.

321. King Albert I of Belgium, himself a pilot, visits the airport of Haren, Brussels, headquarters of SNETA.

322. One of the first real air liners – the 12-seat Handley Page W.8, which won first prize at both the Air Ministry Civil Aviation Competition in 1920 and the International Meeting in Brussels. Afterwards it was used by Handley Page Transport.

323. General 'Billy' Mitchell.

324-5. Fiery disciple of all-out air power, Mitchell achieved fame in September 1918 by marshalling a tremendous force of 1,481 warplanes and flinging them against the Germans during the successful battle for the St. Mihiel salient in France. A firm believer in the big bomber, he ordered Martin MB-2's (*above*), and used them to sink several old German and U.S. battleships at sea in 1921-3. Claiming that this proved the obsolescence of sea power, he crossed swords with senior U.S. officers, was court-martialled in 1925 and suspended from duty. Twenty years later, after his death, he was restored to service with the rank of major general and awarded the Congressional Medal of Honour.

326-7. In Britain air power was sold to the public through the medium of the R.A.F. Display, first held at Hendon in July 1920. Over 60,000 people saw fighters and bombers in action, including Sopwith Snipes (*left*). Counterpart at the 1924 Display (*above*) was a fighter-bomber attack on a dummy ship by Fairey Flycatcher carrier-based fighters.

328. Many ex-military pilots sank their money on war-surplus aircraft and 'barnstormed' across America, giving hair-raising displays of aerobatics, wing-walking and other stunts. Between times they sold joy-rides to the braver members of their audience. Here, according to its 1922 caption, 'Lt. Hardon, the air dare-devil who lost his life, climbs from one plane to another'. A few, more fortunate airmen, managed to scrape a precarious living as stunt pilots during the filming of Hollywood epics such as *Hell's Angels* and *Wings*.

329. Availability of fast, manœuvrable war-surplus aeroplanes made air racing more popular than ever after the 1914–18 War. In July 1921 Cambridge beat Oxford in the first University Air Race. Both teams flew S.E.5 fighters.

330. In 1922 the first of the annual races for the King's Cup, awarded by King George V, was won by Frank Barnard, chief pilot of the Instone Air Line, flying a D.H.4A. His average speed for the 810-mile circuit of Britain was 120 m.p.h.

331. The Schneider Trophy meetings were resumed in 1919, when the contest was declared null and void because of fog. Italy won the next two contests, and needed one more victory in 1922 to win the Trophy outright. Instead, it was regained for Britain by Henri Biard in the Super-marine Sea Lion flying boat, at a speed of 145 62 m.p.h.

332. Only American-built warplanes flown in action by U.S. pilots in the 1914–18 War were D.H.4's with Liberty engines. Curtiss were rightly famous for their JN–4 'Jenny' trainers and large flying boats: but few of the now-famous companies of the U.S. aircraft industry existed before the early 1920's. Typical is Douglas Aircraft, which opened this small factory in Santa Monica, California, in 1920, with a capital of £350. Twenty-three years later Douglas was the largest producer of aircraft in the world, with 16 million square feet of factory space and 160,000 employees.

333. Donald W. Douglas (*left*) working on his first design – the Cloudster – which was the first aircraft to lift its own weight in payload.

334. Boeing's factory in 1922. The aircraft are Boeing MB-3A fighters, designed originally by Thomas-Morse. Altogether 200 were built – the first large U.S. post-war military order.

335. Original Lockheed Company, formed by Allan and Malcolm Lockheed (Loughead) in 1916, built this trim moulded-plywood S-1 sports plane. Far ahead of its day, it could not compete with cheap war-surplus aircraft, and the company suspended manufacture in 1920. Six years later it was re-formed by Allan Lockheed and Jack Northrop.

336. Most revolutionary aircraft of 1920 was Oswald Short's *Silver Streak*, with an all-metal 'monocoque' structure. Not until the Spitfire went into production sixteen years later was this type of construction adopted generally.

337. Wing leading-edge slots, perfected by Sir Frederick Handley Page and Dr. G. V. Lachmann in 1919, were first flown on the H.P.17, a modified D.H.9. By controlling airflow over the wing and so enabling aircraft to fly very slowly under perfect control, they ended the danger of the stall-and-spin type of crash. When adopted for all R.A.F. aircraft, accidents decreased from a total of 54 in 1927 to 31 in 1928. Slots are still used to enable observation aircraft to fly very slowly, and to reduce the landing speed of very fast aeroplanes.

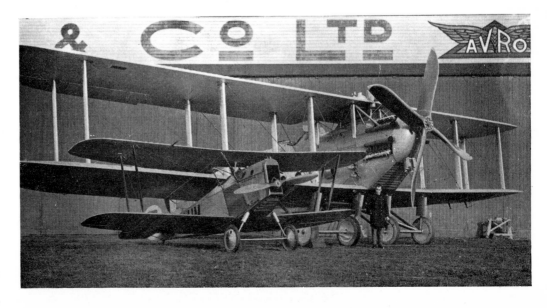

338. World's most powerful aero-engine in 1922 was the 1,000-h.p. Napier Cub tested in this large Avro biplane. Contrast is provided by an Avro Baby, one of the best-known sporting aircraft of the time.

339. Direct services between city centres, now possible only with helicopters, were pioneered in 1921 by a Vickers Viking III amphibian. Carrying Major-General Sir Frederick Sykes, Controller General of Civil Aviation, it flew from the Seine, near the centre of Paris, to the Thames, near the Houses of Parliament, in two hours. Same journey by normal airline service today takes over four hours.

340. Early proof of the value of air freighting was given in May 1919, when a Fairey IIIC operated for a week an experimental newspaper delivery service from the Thames, near Westminster Bridge, to towns on the Kent coast. Customers were able to buy their *Evening News* two hours earlier than usual.

341. Other exploits by Fairey aircraft included the first crossing of the South Atlantic by Captains Sacadura Cabral and Gago Coutinho of the Portuguese Navy. The floats of their Fairey IIIC seaplane were wrecked by high seas at St. Paul's Rocks and another aircraft had to be sent out to them. This too was wrecked at Fernando de Noronha, and they completed their flight on a third. Less troublesome was the flight from Cairo to the Cape and back made in 1926 by four Fairey IIID biplanes (*above*). On their return to Cairo they were fitted with floats and flown to England, making a total of 14,000 miles per aircraft without incident.

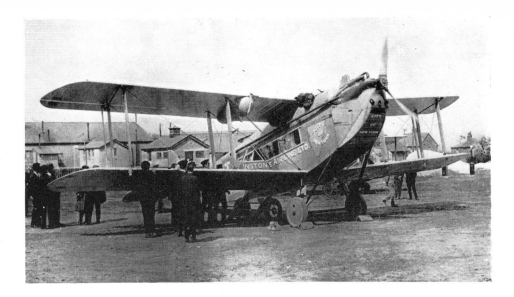

342. Up to 30 cross-Channel services a day were operating to and from London's airport at Croydon by August 1922. The 10-seat D.H.34 *City of New York* flew on Instone's London – Brussels route.

343. Anthony Fokker's air liners, built in Holland, became as famous as his 1914–18 War fighters. This Fokker F.W.3 was owned by a Russian airline.

344. Military flying was banned in Germany by the Treaty of Versailles; but commercial flying was permitted. This Dornier was the first German visitor to Croydon, in 1923.

345–6. New uses were found for aircraft, many of them stunts to catch the headlines and build up public air-mindedness. Horses and dismantled motor cars were carried by freight-planes; rain-making experiments were made by Instone; air ambulance flights were started; Alexandra Roses were flown to the Continent by a decorated aeroplane and half a ton of mince-pies air-lifted in another. In June 1927 a Handley Page W.8 (*above*) was fitted out to photograph the eclipse of the sun, above clouds that might have obscured it from cameras on the ground.

347. Main tasks of aircraft builders and operators in the 'twenties were to persuade governments to buy new warplanes, when there were still thousands of war-surplus fighters and bombers in store, and to build up air-mindedness in the public. Britain's Gloucestershire (Gloster) Company designed, built and flew their little Mars I racer in three weeks, as the prototype for a new fighter. It won the Aerial Derby in 1921, 1922 and 1923, set up a British Speed Record of 196·6 m.p.h., and helped to persuade the Air Ministry to order a whole series of Gloster fighters for the R.A.F.

348. In America Army and Navy pilots battled for the Pulitzer Trophy each year from 1920 to 1925. Except in the first contest, the winners all flew Curtiss racers, with powerful Curtiss liquid-cooled engines that made possible new concepts of streamlining. This Curtiss R3C-1 won the 1925 Pulitzer race for the U.S. Army. A few days later, on floats, it was flown to victory in the Schneider Trophy contest at Baltimore by Lt. 'Jimmy' Doolittle, at a speed of 232.5 m.p.h.

349. One of the greatest of the long-distance fliers who pioneered world air routes in the 'twenties was Alan Cobham. When the four struggling British private airlines were combined in the Government-subsidised Imperial Airways in 1924 he flew the Director of Civil Aviation, Sir Sefton Brancker (with topee), to Rangoon and back in a Puma-engined D.H.50 belonging to the new airline. Brancker did much for British commercial flying, before he was killed in the crash of the airship R.101 in 1930.

350. First successful round-the-world flight was made by pilots of the U.S. Air Service in 1924. They flew specially-built Douglas World Cruisers, powered by 400-h.p. Liberty engines and with alternative wheel or float undercarriages.

351. Named after the U.S. cities of Seattle, Chicago, Boston and New Orleans, the four World Cruisers took off from Lake Washington, Seattle, on 6th April 1924. *Seattle* hit a mountainside in Alaska. *Boston* force-landed in the Atlantic. The other two arrived back at Seattle on 28th September after a 27,534-mile flight over 28 countries.

352. Early mountain pilot was François Durafour of Geneva, who made the first landing and take-off on Mont-Blanc, at a height of 14,000 ft., in a Caudron biplane, on 30th July 1921.

353. On 2nd–3rd May 1923 Lts. Macready and Kelly made the first non-stop coast-to-coast flight across North America, from New York to San Diego, in 26 hours 50 minutes in a Fokker T-2.

354. This Jaguar-engined D.H.50 was used by Alan Cobham for his famous flights to Capetown and back and Australia and back in 1925–6. Blazing a trial for Imperial Airways to follow, they earned him a knighthood.

355. Another great survey flight was made in 1925 by Edmond Thieffry, who linked Belgium with the Congo for the first time in this three-engined Handley Page Hamilton, named after Princess Marie-José of the Belgians.

356. (*Right*) Edmond Thieffry was given a terrific welcome in Brussels, after his pioneer 5,000-mile flight to the Congo.

357. Last of Cobham's survey flights was a 23,000-mile circuit of Africa in 1927 in a Short Singapore flying boat (*left*). Landing at places where no aeroplane had ever before been seen, he proved the ability of flying boats to operate without the prepared airfields and equipment needed by landplanes. Imperial Airways ordered three Short Calcutta flying boats, developed from the Singapore, for the Mediterranean section of their Croydon–India service, and became more and more flying boat minded in the next ten years.

358. After completing his series of long-distance survey flights, Sir Alan Cobham (*below*) organised the National Aviation Day 'air circus' which toured the British Isles 1932–5. He also perfected the technique of refuelling in flight.

359. Achievement which captured the imagination of the public more than any other was the first non-stop New York–Paris flight by 24-year-old American Charles Lindbergh on 20th–21st May 1927. Flying alone, in the small Ryan monoplane, *Spirit of St. Louis*, with a single engine of only 220-h.p., he covered the 3,600 miles in 33½ hours, was mobbed by vast crowds after landing at Le Bourget, Paris, and fêted for weeks afterwards in France, Britain and the United States.

360. Lindbergh, here with his mother, had a hard schooling for the Atlantic flight as a U.S. Mail Service pilot. Twice he had to escape by parachute when his ancient mailplanes ran out of fuel in bad weather.

361. The great Australian pilot, Sir Charles Kingsford Smith, first to fly the Pacific and the 1,400-mile Tasman Sea, disappeared whilst attempting to break the England–Australia record in 1935.

362. *Southern Cross*, the Fokker F.VIIb monoplane in which Kingsford Smith made the first flight across the Pacific, 31st May to 9th June 1928. The route from San Fancisco to Brisbane, via Honolulu and Fiji, totalled 6,850 miles. Co-pilot was fellow-Australian Charles Ulm, who also accompanied 'Smithy' on the first flight across the Tasman Sea in *Southern Cross* in September 1928, and later flights.

363. An attempt to fly to the North Pole was made by the Swedish explorer Andrée and two companions in 1897. They died after their balloon was forced down in the Arctic. First successful flight over the Pole was made on 9th May, 1926, by Lt.-Cdr. (later Rear-Admiral) Richard Byrd, in the trimotor Fokker *Josephine Ford* (*left*), piloted by Floyd Bennett. Soon afterwards Bennett died, but when Byrd flew over the South Pole on 28th November 1929 he named his Ford monoplane *Floyd Bennett*. Its pilot was Bernt Balchen, probably the greatest Arctic flier of all time.

364. Byrd's greatest rival in the race to be first over the North Pole was the Norwegian explorer Roald Amundsen, who had tried to reach the Pole in a Dornier Wal flying boat of this type in 1925.

365. Amundsen's airship, the *Norge*, circled the North Pole for two hours of scientific observation on 11th May 1926 – just two days after Byrd had flown over it.

366. Many great flights were made by Royal Air Force flying boats in the 1920's, for training and to 'show the flag'. These Supermarine Southamptons flew to Egypt and back in 1926. Next year, four more, led by Group Captain H. M. Cave-Brown-Cave, completed a 23,000-mile cruise in formation from Plymouth to Singapore, around the Australian Continent and on to Japan before returning to their base at Singapore. The same aircraft flew to Calcutta and back in 1929 to survey part of the proposed Empire air route to Australia.

367. A great milestone in aviation history was the first flight of Juan de la Cierva's C-4 Autogiro at Madrid, Spain, on 9th January 1923. First practical rotating wing aircraft, it offered hope of improved safety, by eliminating long landing and take-off runs. This later Autogiro was tested in England in 1926.

368. Technique of flight refuelling, to increase aircraft range, was pioneered by the U.S. Air Service in the summer of 1923. Repeated refuellings by a 'flying tanker' enabled Lts. L. H. Smith and J. P. Richter to remain airborne for over 37 hours in their D.H.4, over San Diego.

369. Greatly improved performance followed the perfection of metal propellers by Dr. Albert Reed. Fairey Aviation bought the licence to manufacture both the 'streamlined' Curtiss engine and Reed's propeller in England, fitted them in its Fox bomber, and advanced the speed of R.A.F. day bombers by 50 m.p.h.

370–1. Still intent on encouraging British aviation progress, the *Daily Mail* offered a prize of £1,000 in 1923 for a 'motor glider' competition. The Duke of Sutherland offered £500 for the longest flight on one gallon of petrol in an aeroplane with an engine of not more than 750 c.c. capacity. So the Royal Aero Club organised a Light Aeroplane Competition at Lympne in Kent. Joint winners of the main prize were Walter Longton in the English Electric Wren (*left*), and Jimmy James in W. S. Shackleton's A.N.E.C. (*below*). Both covered 87½ miles on one gallon of petrol.

372. In January 1924 the Air Ministry offered a prize of £3,000 for a competition for two-seat light-planes with engines not exceeding 1,100 c.c. Winner this time was the Beardmore Wee Bee, also designed by Shackleton. Two years later, a new *Daily Mail* Light Aeroplane Competition at Lympne was won by this Hawker Cygnet (*below*), which is still airworthy after 30 years. Powered by a 36-h.p. Bristol Cherub engine, it has a top speed of 80 m.p.h.

373–4. Air Ministry interest in lightplanes was directed at finding a suitable aircraft for Flying Clubs, which were to receive official subsidy. De Havilland's entered their single-seat Humming Bird (*right*) for the 1923 Light Aeroplane Competition. Realising that a more practical two-seater was required, they built a small biplane, with a 60-h.p. Cirrus engine. Named the Moth (*below*), this aircraft made its first flight in February 1925, and was an immediate success. The Air Ministry ordered it into production for the Flying Clubs and it started a boom in private and club flying that spread across the world.

375. The Moth could be bought for £595, flown by almost anybody, towed behind a car and kept in a garage. Three years later it even had its own engine – the 80-h.p. Gipsy, designed by Frank Halford – which increased its speed to 95 m.p.h.

376. Amy Johnson with *Jason*, the Moth which she flew solo from England to Australia in 1930. It can still be seen in the National Aeronautical Collection in South Kensington.

377. Following the trail blazed by Cobham, Kingsford Smith and the Royal Air Force, Imperial Airways pushed their Empire Air Routes further and further from Britain. On 20th December 1926 the first of the airline's new de Havilland Hercules air liners, designed for the England–India service, left on its proving flight to Delhi, where it was named *City of Delhi* by the Viceroy, Lord Irwin. Unfortunately, the Persians refused to allow foreign aircraft to fly over their country; so passengers could be flown at first only as far as Basra, where they were transferred to ships.

378. Another fine air liner introduced into service with Imperial Airways in 1926 was the Armstrong Whitworth Argosy. One of these aircraft, the *City of Glasgow*, left Croydon on 31st March 1929 with the first air mail for India.

379. Arrival of H.R.H. the Prince of Wales at Croydon, by Imperial Airways Argosy, 26th March, 1929. A keen air traveller, the Prince owned several lightplanes, in which he flew regularly with his personal pilot, Flt.-Lt. Fielden. When he became King Edward VIII in 1936 he appointed Fielden Captain of the King's Flight.

380. Greatest of all the landplane air liners flown by Imperial Airways were the eight H.P.42 Hannibal-class biplanes. With a speed of under 100 m.p.h., they were accused of having built-in headwinds; but in the 1930's they carried more passengers between London and the Continent than all other air liners combined. This photograph shows *Helena* at Croydon.

381. Night scene at Croydon, 1931. There were two versions of the H.P.42. *Heracles*, shown here, was an 'Eastern' machine, designed for operation in semi-tropical conditions on the long mail routes between Karachi, Cairo and Kisumu. The H.P.42 offered passengers pullman-class luxury, with full course hot meals. They also introduced enclosed cockpits for the crew, who promptly exchanged their leather flying suits and goggles for blue serge uniforms, gold braid and peaked caps. Together, they flew about 10 million miles, without ever hurting a passenger, until the last of them disappeared during a wartime flight in 1940.

382. First four-motor monoplanes used by Imperial Airways were the Armstrong Whitworth Atalanta class, introduced in 1933 on services from Central Africa to Capetown and through Karachi, Calcutta and Rangoon to Singapore.

383. From the start Imperial Airways' aim was to operate only multi-engined aircraft, and to use flying boats for long over-water stages. Some of the fleet of Short Calcutta and Kent 'boats used on the airline's Mediterranean and Cairo–M'wanza routes are shown here at Alexandria.

384. Other airlines too were expanding. Air Union's 1929 fleet, based at Le Bourget, Paris, included Leo 21 (F-AIFE), Blériot 165 (F-AIKI), Breguet 280T (F-AJAN) and Farman Goliath multi-engined air liners.

385. Progress in America was still slow. Commercial air transportation did not start until 6th April 1926, when Varney Air Lines began operating the first privately-contracted air mail service between Pasco, Washington, and Elko, Nevada. First pouch of mail was brought to the airport by stagecoach.

386. Pilot on Varney's first air-mail flight was Leon D. Cuddeback. Aircraft used was a single-engined, open-cockpit Swallow biplane.

387. To mark the inauguration of air-freight carrying at Chicago, 1st September 1927, a 10-gallon stetson hat was flown to comedian Will Rogers by National Air Transport.

388. After winning the contract to carry mail over the 1,918-mile Chicago–San Francisco route, Boeing designed and built a fleet of 25 Model 40A mail planes in five months. Their enclosed cabins and heated cockpits made possible the first regular transcontinental air passenger service by Boeing Air Transport which, like Varney Air Lines and National Air Transport, later became part of United Air Lines' 13,250-mile network.

389. Passengers boarding a Boeing 40B-4 air liner of Pacific Air Transport, another predecessor of United Air Lines.

390. First airline stewardesses were these eight young nurses hired by Boeing Air Transport on 15th May, 1930, to serve aboard its San Francisco-Chicago aircraft.

391. In-flight meals for passengers aboard National Air Transport's Ford tri-motors in 1930 consisted of sandwiches wrapped in wax paper with the addition of the unspecified beverages here being handed round.

392. Using the moulded plywood construction featured on their 1920 Model S-1 Sportsplane, Lockheed built a series of very fast, 'clean' monoplanes in the late 1920's and early 1930's. Typical was the six-seat Orion, used by Varney Air Lines, and which could fly at 225 m.p.h. Powered by a 420-h.p. Pratt and Whitney Wasp engine, it was the first commercial aircraft with an efficient retractable undercarriage.

393. The Royal Navy continued to develop the aircraft carrier after the 1914–18 War. Main problem was to find a safe method of landing-on. The rear flight deck on H.M.S. *Furious* was only half an answer, as air currents around the vessel's bridge and funnel made accurate flying impossible. Experiments with dummy superstructures on H.M.S. *Argus*, which normally had a completely clear deck from bow to stem, showed that the now-familiar 'island' on the starboard side was the most satisfactory arrangement for bridge and funnel. For a time arrester wires were dispensed with entirely on the long decks of the Royal Navy's newer carriers *Eagle* and *Hermes*. Later, when landing speeds increased, the modern system of transverse wires was perfected. America's first carrier, the *Langley* (*right*) followed the layout of *Argus*, with no superstructure. Commissioned in March 1922, she had a 534-foot-long flight deck, was equipped with Vought VE-7 and Aeromarine training aircraft.

394. Never losing its faith in the carrier-based torpedo-bomber as the major weapon of sea-air warfare, the Royal Navy followed the Sopwith Cuckoo with the improved Blackburn Dart and Ripon (*above*). The Fleet Air Arm was still part of the Royal Air Force; but, from 1924, after being trained by the R.A.F., pilots went to sea as permanent naval pilots. Result was greatly improved morale.

395. To supplement aircraft carriers, limited by the Washington Naval Treaty, most large warships carried reconnaissance seaplanes, which were catapult-launched. Standard U.S. shipborne seaplane for many years was the Vought O2U-1 Corsair, with Pratt and Whitney Wasp engine. Power and reliability of Wasp and Curtiss-Wright Cyclone air-cooled radial engines caused the U.S. to neglect more streamlined liquid-cooled engines in the 'thirties.

396. Main supplier of British naval aircraft for more than 40 years was The Fairey Aviation Company. Here the famed Fairey Flycatcher fighter of the 'twenties is seen over its floating airfield, H.M.S. *Hermes*.

397. Overseas, the Royal Air Force struggled on with 1914–18 War aircraft for ten years after the Armistice. Backbone of its forces sent to maintain order in the Middle East and N.W. Frontier of India was the D.H.9 bomber. This one was modified into a pioneer air ambulance during fighting in Somaliland, 1920. A stretcher was carried under a lid on its rear fuselage.

398. D.H.9A of No. 8 Squadron, R.A.F., over Baghdad, 1926. Four years earlier the R.A.F. had been made entirely responsible for maintenance of peace and order in Iraq, where eight assorted squadrons did the job of an army. Equipped largely with D.H.9A's, supported by one squadron of fighters and two of Vickers Vernon troop transports, this force waged a continuous battle against rebel tribes.

399. Successive Vickers transports of 1920's and 1930's–the Vimy, Vernon and Victoria (right) – flew troops from one trouble spot to another in the Middle East, took a hand in the fighting as 'heavy bombers' when necessary.

400. Air Ministry decision in 1926, to switch to metal construction for all new aircraft led to gradual re-equipment of squadrons with Bulldog and Siskin fighters; Hinaidi, Virginia, Side-strand, Wapiti and IIIF bombers. These Siskins (below) carry the insignia of No. 29 Squadron, based at North Weald, Essex, in 1932.

401.   British super-bomber of 1928 was the all-metal Beardmore Inflexible, powered by three 650-h.p. Rolls-Royce Condor engines. Too advanced for its day, it did not go into service.

402–3.   This was the golden age of biplanes. Fast, manœuvrable single-seat fighters like the Boeing P-12E (*left*) and Bristol Bulldog (*below*), thrilled air-display crowds with formation aerobatics and 250 m.p.h. power-dives; and made rings round the lumbering heavy bombers of their day. But their level speed was only 175–190 m.p.h. at a time when Supermarine Schneider Trophy racers were hitting over 400 m.p.h., and they still carried the 1914–18 War armament of two machine-guns.

404. Zeppelin was still a name to be respected, thanks to the efforts of Dr. Hugo Eckener, greatest airship pilot of all time. He raised money to build the 772-ft.-long *Graf Zeppelin* which, in 1928, made the first of over 100 transatlantic flights, from Friedrichshafen, Germany, to Lakehurst, New York, carrying a crew of 40 and 20 passengers. In 1929 it made a round-the-world goodwill flight of 21,500 miles in 20 days.

405. Everest was conquered for the first time on 3rd April 1933, when two Westland biplanes of the Houston-Everest Expedition flew over the world's highest mountain and photographed its summit from a height of 34,000 feet.

406. Great flights and great aircraft grace every page of the story of aviation progress in the 'thirties. Short's Sarafand flying boat of 1932 was the largest aircraft then built in Britain. Powered by six 820-h.p. Rolls-Royce Buzzards, it weighed 31 tons, could cruise for 1,450 miles at 150 m.p.h.

407. Even bigger than the Sarafand, Germany's Dornier Do-X needed twelve engines to lift it off the water. Powered initially by 550-h.p. Siemens radials, it was later re-engined with 615-h.p. Curtiss Conquerors, which gave it a top speed of 130 m.p.h. The Do-X weighed 55 tons and could carry 169 passengers. During a visit to England in 1930 it was piloted for 10 minutes by the Prince of Wales. Later, it flew to New York and back.

408. Landplane counterpart of Do-X was the Junkers G.38 *Generalfeldmarschall von Hindenburgh*. Largest landplane in the world, it weighed 20 tons and had four 600-h.p. Jumo diesel engines buried inside its huge 150-ft. span wings.

409. (*Below*) At the other end of the size scale was the first of the Granville brothers' Gee Bee racers, the Sportster D of 1930, here dwarfed by a twin-engined Curtiss Condor air liner. A 125-h.p. Menasco engine gave the Sportster a top speed of 159 m.p.h. – about the same as the 1,200 h.p. Condor.

410. (*Above*) Last and greatest of the Gee Bees was the 7–11 Super Sportster in which 'Jimmy' Doolittle won the 1932 race for the Thompson Trophy. Only 17 ft. 9 in. long, this fantastic aircraft could fly at over 300 m.p.h., with a 535-h.p. Wasp engine.

411. Eighteen years of fierce international rivalry in contests for the Schneider Trophy (*left*) ended in 1931 when Britain won the Trophy outright.

412. Architect of victory was R. J. Mitchell, chief designer of the Supermarine Company. He realised in 1923 that the key to success was the cleanest possible monoplane design fitted with the most powerful engine available.

413. Mitchell's first monoplane racer was the S.4, which set a new world seaplane speed record of 226 m.p.h., but developed wing flutter and crashed before it could compete in the 1925 Schneider contest.

414. Two years later, the more sturdy Supermarine S.5 won the contest at Venice with a speed of 281·65 m.p.h. From it was developed the S.6, winner of the 1929 contest, and the S.6B, which gave Britain her third successive win in 1931.

415.   Pilot of the Supermarine S.6B, which won the Trophy outright, was Flt.-Lt. John Boothman, whose speed over the 189-mile course at Ryde, Isle of Wight, was 340·6 m.p.h.

416.   On 29th September, 1931, 16 days after the Schneider victory, Flt.-Lt. G. H. Stainforth set up a new world speed record of 407 m.p.h. in the second S.6B.

417.   Supermarine S.6 at Calshot, 1929. The Air Ministry had begun to realise the value of air racing as a means of developing and proving new ideas on design, new engines and equipment in 1924. They financed the Schneider racers until 1929, when they decided the cost was too high to continue. Two years later, at the last minute, Lady Houston provided the cash which enabled Britain to win the all-important third successive victory. Pilots of the winning machines in 1927, 1929 and 1931 were members of the specially-formed R.A.F. High Speed Flight.

418.   To profit from design experience gained in the Schneider contests, the Air Ministry ordered from Supermarine a single-seat fighter, to Specification F7/30. The Specification was too restrictive and, although Mitchell's fighter shared the graceful fuselage lines of his racers, it had a speed of only 230 m.p.h. Believing he could produce a world-beater if given a free hand, Mitchell started work on a new fighter, built around the promising Rolls-Royce PV–12 engine. It was destined to win immortal fame as the Spitfire.

419–20. Every week seemed to bring some new aviation record, made possible by aircraft like Lockheed's five-seat, 220-h.p. Vega, named after the brightest star in the heavens. In 1931 a Vega was flown around the world in 8 days 15 hours 51 minutes by Wiley Post (*right*) and Harold Gatty. Two years later, Post made the first solo flight around the world in the Vega *Winnie Mae*, covering 15,596 miles in 7 days 18 hours 50 minutes. The undercarriage could be jettisoned to increase speed. He was later killed in a crash, with comedian Will Rogers.

421. Col. Lindbergh with his wife Anne, made a trans-Pacific goodwill flight and a 30,000-mile tour to Europe and South America.

422. The Blériot-Zappata 110 was ordered by the French Air Ministry for record-breaking flights. In December 1930, piloted by Bossoutrot and Rossi, it raised the world duration record to 67 hours 53 minutes. Fifteen months later the same crew set up a closed-circuit distance record of 6,703 miles. In August 1933 Codos and Rossi flew non-stop from New York to Rayak, Syria, establishing a straight-line distance record of 5,654 miles.

423. In 1931 the Italian Air Minister, General Italo Balbo, led a mass flight of 12 Savoia-Marchetti flying boats across the South Atlantic from Rome to Brazil. Two years later he led an even greater armada of 24 flying boats across the North Atlantic and back. Neither flight was achieved without loss of life; but they gave a remarkable demonstration of the growing reliability and possibilities of aviation.

424. *Heart's Content*, the de Havilland Puss Moth in which Jim Mollison flew the North Atlantic, from Ireland to New Brunswick, at a petrol and oil cost of £11 1s. 3d. in August 1932. The Australian pilot, Bert Hinkler, had used a similar aircraft for the first west–east crossing of the South Atlantic in 1931.

425. World long-distance record was gained for Britain for the first time on 6–8th February 1933 by Squad.-Ldr. O. R. Gayford and Flt.-Lieut. Nicholetts, who flew 5,309 miles non-stop from Cranwell to Walvis Bay, South Africa, in this Fairey Long Range Monoplane.

426. With a unique Fiat 24-cylinder 'double' engine developing 3,100 h.p., Italy's Macchi MC-72 seaplane was too late for the 1931 Schneider Trophy contest. On 23rd October 1934, piloted by Warrant-Officer F. Agello, it set up a world speed record of 440·7 m.p.h., which still stands as a seaplane record.

427. Following in the tradition of Amy Johnson, women pilots made several remarkable record flights in the 1930's. Jean Batten (*above*) flew solo from England to Australia in a Moth in 1934; to South America in a Percival Gull in 1935; and to her homeland, New Zealand, in 1936, also in a Gull.

428. First woman to fly the Atlantic as a passenger was Amelia Earhart of America. Four years later she became the first woman to make a solo transatlantic flight.

429.   Designed as a sturdy, simple 'twin-engined Moth', the de Havilland Dragon began to make money for Britain's small independent airline operators in 1933. One was bought by the Prince of Wales and decorated in the red and blue colours of the Household Brigade Flying Club. The cleaned-up Dragon Rapide is still widely used.

430.   First of the famous Taylor Cubs appeared in 1931. From it have been developed all the Cub and Auster lightplanes of today.

431.   In Britain, in 1933, F. G. Miles marketed his neat two-seat Hawk for £395. It was followed by many other, equally successful Miles lightplanes, racers and trainers.

432. Heinkel produced the fast and beautiful He.70 transport, which, like many other German civil aircraft of the 'thirties, proved easily convertible into a bomber when the existence of the *Luftwaffe* was announced by Hitler in 1935.

433. First all-metal streamlined monoplane air liner built in America was the Boeing 247 of 1933. Powered by two 550-h.p. Wasps, it was the first twin-engined monoplane able to climb on one engine with a full load, and introduced refinements such as control surface trim tabs, automatic pilot and de-icing equipment. It reduced the U.S. transcontinental flight time to under 20 hours with 10 passengers.

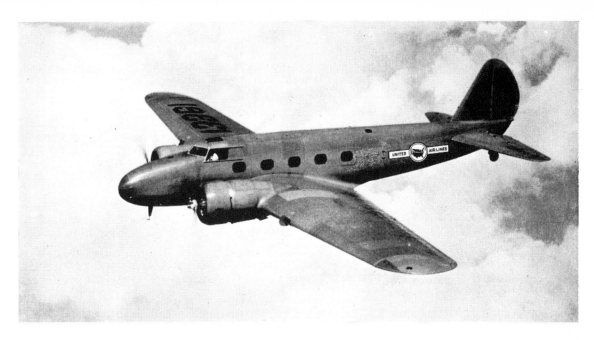

434. Famous 9,000-mile Christmas mail flight was made by the K.L.M. Fokker F-XVIII *Pelikaan*, which left Amsterdam on 18th December 1933 and reached Jakarta four days later.

435. Last link in the air-mail service from Britain to Australia was forged in 1934, when the Australian Qantas company began flying mail from Singapore to Brisbane in D.H.86 transports.

436. Outstanding aviation event of 1934 was the great MacRobertson Air Race from Mildenhall, England, to Melbourne, Australia. Winners were C. W. A. Scott and T. Campbell Black in a specially-designed de Havilland Comet racer. They brought Australia within three days' flying time of England for the first time.

Return of the Monoplane

WHEN Scott and Black landed their little red monoplane racer at Melbourne, 71 hours and 18 seconds after leaving England, they did more than win a race. They drove the final nail into the coffin of the biplane. Their de Havilland Comet was designed and built specially for the MacRobertson Air Race, and nothing like it had been seen before. Its two Gipsy Six engines gave a total of only 460 h.p.; yet careful streamlining, removal of every ounce of unnecessary weight and the use of a retractable undercarriage gave it a top speed of 237 m.p.h.

It was impressive – and so was the performance of K.L.M.'s Douglas D.C.2 monoplane air liner, which won the handicap section of the race, carrying a full load of passengers. Its crew, Captains Parmentier and Moll, stepped from their cockpit smiling and clad in spotless white uniforms, in contrast with the dishevelled, exhausted Scott and Black.

What the D.C.2 had done, other air liners could and would do again and again, until it was commonplace. Long-distance flying was no longer a hazardous sport for supermen in freak aircraft. It was a business. The aeroplane had grown up, and the monoplane, with its higher speed and better payload, had made it possible.

In America the D.C.2 was followed by the D.C.3, destined for immortal fame as the Dakota – workhorse of almost every airline and air force in the world. In Britain Imperial Airways ordered a new fleet of 28 Short monoplane flying boats, to be used *exclusively* on all their Empire routes. It was an unprecedented gamble, because the order was placed while the design was still on the drawing-board, despite the fact that they were to be the first four-engined all-metal monoplane 'boats ever built, and there was no evidence that a large fleet of flying boats could be operated successfully.

History proved that the gamble was justified, for the Empire 'boats between them covered eventually well over 40 million miles. The first, *Canopus*, flew on 4th July 1936. Less than four months later she was in regular passenger service on Imperial Airways' trans-Mediterranean run.

With her sister-ships, she gave Britain a leadership on the world's civil air routes such as she had never know before and is unlikely ever to recapture. As a start, the Empire 'boats were used to inaugurate the Empire Air Mail scheme, by which all letters and postcards from Britain to any part of the Empire were carried at a rate of $1\frac{1}{2}d.$ per half-ounce, one-sixteenth of the cost of a half-ounce air-mail letter to Australia today.

Next, in 1937, *Caledonia* and *Cambria* were adapted to make the first east–west airline flights across the North Atlantic; while the Pan American Airways flying boat *Clipper III* made a simultaneous pioneer west–east crossing.

It seemed that the golden age of air travel was about to begin, and that flying boats would be supreme for long-distance over-water services. Even private flying was becoming more popular, thanks to Government schemes such as the

British Civil Air Guard, designed to enable any willing and able young man or woman to learn to fly.

The C.A.G. was really a sign of the times; for its purpose was to build up a reserve of pilots to reinforce the fighting Services in any future war. There seemed little doubt that war would come and, from 1936, Britain's aircraft industry had been redoubling its efforts to produce monoplane fighters and bombers to match the Me.109 fighters, Dornier Do.17, Heinkel He.111 and Junkers Ju.87 bombers of Hitler's new *Luftwaffe*.

The aircraft they built were good. Sydney Camm's Hurricane, the world's first eight-gun monoplane fighter, was entering service in considerable numbers by 1939. Hard on its heels followed the Spitfire, last and greatest design of R. J. Mitchell, who died soon after the prototype flew. Fairey Battle, Bristol Blenheim, Vickers Wellington and Handley Page Hampden bombers were all in large-scale production; so were Lysander army co-operation aircraft, Anson patrol-bombers, Sunderland flying boats and other modern aircraft. To supplement the efforts of the aircraft industry vast new 'shadow factories' were built, and the motor manufacturers were called in to run some of them.

By 1939 the Royal Air Force was beginning to look very different from the ancient and tattered collection of biplanes that had been inspected by King George V at his Jubilee Review of the R.A.F. in 1935.

Even more important things were happening behind the scenes. Lofty aerials began to appear at isolated spots on the S.E. coast; but very few people knew that they were the outward and visible signs that Britain's defences had been strengthened immeasurably by the invisible, ever-watching eyes and ears of radio-location, later to be known as radar. Still fewer knew that as early as 1936 the Air Ministry had issued specifications for powerful new four-motor bombers that would produce in due course the mighty Stirlings, Halifaxes and Lancasters which spearheaded Bomber Command in its most glorious and tragic years. And only a handful of men in Britain and Germany knew that the first jet-engines were already running in test houses, and being groomed for the day when they would revolutionise air warfare.

There was plenty of evidence of the part that air power would play in a future war. Mussolini's 'eagles' had won glory in Abyssinia by dropping high-explosive and mustard-gas bombs on poorly armed tribesmen. In Spain the latest Italian and German fighters and bombers, flown by men of the *Regia Aeronautica* and *Luftwaffe*, fought with the armies of General Franco against fighters and bombers from Russia. The new technique of ground attack by fighters was perfected, and the world saw with horror something of the power of the bomber when the village of Guernica was destroyed, allegedly in error, by pilots of the German Condor Legion.

When World War II started on 3rd September 1939 aviation still meant little more to the average man or woman than a five-bob joy-ride at Alan Cobham's Air Circus, or a means of getting a letter from Aunt Matilda in Sydney in one week instead of six. Like Flanagan and Allen, on a favourite gramophone record, they were still 'on the outside, always looking in'; and, for most of them, aeroplanes were merely remote, silver shapes they sometimes saw silhouetted against a summer sky.

Unfortunately, the summer was over, the silver shapes assumed a dark mantle of military camouflage, and aviation became a matter of life and death for the men, women and children of half the world.

437–9. Air power was born in the early 1930's, with the appearance of the first efficient long-range monoplane bombers. From the start, the pace was set by the American Boeing Company, whose five-seat all-metal Y1B-9 (*above*) had a range of 1,250 miles with a ton of bombs. Then, in 1934, came the Martin B-10B (*left*), representing the greatest single advance in bomber development since the Handley Page 0/400 of the First World War. Its speed of 212 m.p.h. enabled it to outfly most fighters of its day and it introduced refinements such as retractable undercarriage, enclosed cockpit and internal bomb-bay. The four-engined Boeing Y1B-17 (*below*) was received with less enthusiasm. U.S. Air Corps experts preferred to carry their high-explosive eggs in more, less costly, baskets. Yet this was the prototype of the famous Flying Fortresses which, a few years later, filled the skies over Europe with the thunder of their 1,200-h.p. engines.

440. Germany, barred from building warplanes by the Versailles Treaty, continued to develop high-performance sporting, mail and transport aircraft. Typical were the Heinkel He.51's (*right*), which were as fast and manœuvrable as contemporary British and American fighters. In fact, they were fighters, as the world discovered when Hitler revealed the existence of the powerful new *Luftwaffe* in 1935. Suddenly aware of the consequences of neglecting air power for 15 years, the British Government ordered a panic expansion of the Royal Air Force. France decided to nationalize her aircraft industry, the output of which promptly slumped to negligible proportions.

441. First bombers of the new *Luftwaffe* were three-motor Junkers Ju.52's, easily adapted from the civil air-liner version by the addition of gun positions and bomb-racks.

442-3. Conversion of the Junkers Ju.86 transport (*left*) into the Ju.86K bomber (*right*) was typical of the way Germany planned its secret *Luftwaffe*. Pilots for the fighter squadrons went to Italy as civilians, changed into Italian uniform and trained with the *Regia Aeronautica*.

444. The Spanish Civil War gave the German and Italian Air Forces an excuse to test their new weapons and training methods in action. Pilots of the German Condor Legion first flew He.51's; later re-equipped with Messerschmitt Me.109's (*above*), which were faster and more heavily armed than their opponents, consisting largely of older Russian and French types. The He.51's were switched to ground attack.

445. Franco's air offensive was spearheaded by Italian Savoia-Marchetti S.M.79 bombers, which usually flew fast and high enough to escape any form of counter-attack. German Ju.52's were used to fly Moroccan troops from North Africa, and for bombing, until replaced by more advanced Heinkel He.111's and Dornier Do.17's.

446. Best Republican fighter was the tubby little Russian-built I-16 Rata. Known in Spain as the Mosca 'Fly', it was said to be based on the design of American Gee Bee racing planes. A licence-built Wright Cyclone of 700 h.p. gave it a top speed of 280 m.p.h.

447. Another Russian-built fighter used in Spain in large numbers was the I-15 Chato, also with a Cyclone engine, and armed with four machine-guns. Many were lost when their wings came off during combat manœuvres; and Russia began designing new, better aircraft following war experience in Spain and, later, against Finland.

448. Britain's standard heavy bomber in 1935, when the *Luftwaffe* emerged from secrecy, was the Heyford biplane. Two 640-h.p. Kestrel engines enabled it to carry a heavy bomb-load 2,000 miles; but its top speed was only 142 m.p.h.

449. Latest R.A.F. fighter was the Gloster Gauntlet, a highly manœuvrable little biplane with a 645-h.p. Mercury engine and top speed of 228 m.p.h. From it was developed the faster Gladiator biplane, which entered service in 1936.

450. When Britain's air force was put on show at the 1937 Hendon Air Display, critics implied that little progress had been made since the days of the 20-year-old Horace Farman which flew overhead. Most R.A.F. aircraft were still biplanes, and there was good reason for anxiety over reports of modern aircraft in action in Spain.

451. Proof of the capabilities of Britain's aircraft industry was given by the Bristol 142, ordered by Lord Rothermere as his personal high-speed transport. When sent to the R.A.F. Station at Martlesham Heath for Certificate of Airworthiness trials, the Air Ministry were staggered to discover it would fly at 307 m.p.h. – 100 m.p.h. faster than the R.A.F.'s latest fighters. Asked to loan it for extended tests, Lord Rothermere presented it to the nation, naming it *Britain First*; and the Air Ministry quickly ordered it into production as the Blenheim bomber.

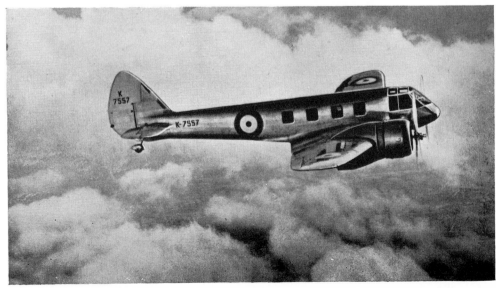

452. World's first 8-gun monoplane fighter – the Hurricane – was designed by Sir Sydney Camm, and later earned him the title of 'the man who saved Britain'.

453. Flown on 6th November 1935, the Hawker Hurricane was first of a new generation of fast, heavily-armed monoplane interceptors. Rolls-Royce's superb 1,030-h.p. Merlin engine gave it a speed of 325 m.p.h. at over 20,000 ft. Sturdy design enabled later versions to carry bombs, rockets and even two anti-tank guns under their wings.

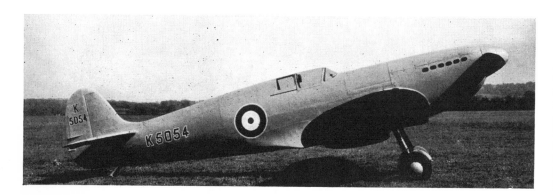

454. Team-mate for the Hurricane was R. J. Mitchell's last and greatest design – the Spitfire. Monocoque construction and new-type wings gave it a higher performance than the Hurricane but delayed production. Powered by a Merlin and armed with eight machine-guns, the production Spitfire Mk.1 had a top speed of 367 m.p.h.

455. Long production lines of Battle day bombers in Fairey's Stockport factory reflected the enthusiasm with which Britain's aircraft and motor industries began equipping the R.A.F. with the modern fighters and bombers it so badly needed. Behind the scenes, Air Ministry strategists planned a new class of formidable four-engined heavy bombers.

456. War seemed inevitable; but its threat did not prevent tremendous progress in civil aviation. As revolutionary as the Martin B-10 bomber was the twin-engined DC-1, which marked the start of the whole long line of successful Douglas air liners. It set a transcontinental record by flying from Los Angeles to New York in 11 hr. 5 min., and was followed by the improved DC-2 (*right*) and DC-3 Dakota.

457. With the air routes of the world opened up by reliable engines and monoplane efficiency, airlines turned more and more to flying boats for long over-water services. Even the North Atlantic no longer held its old terrors, and on 5–6th July 1937 the first airline crossings were made simultaneously by the Sikorsky S-42 *Clipper III* of Pan American Airways from west to east, and by the Short Empire 'boat *Caledonia* of Imperial Airways from east to west. They carried no payload. In the following year the first of Pan American's fine Boeing 314 *Clippers* (*above*) was delivered.

458. Imperial Airways took the biggest gamble in airline history when they ordered twenty-eight Empire flying boats 'off the drawing board' in 1934. The first, *Canopus*, entered regular service four months after its first flight and, with its sisters, gave Britain world leadership in commercial aviation.

459. By refuelling in mid-air, from Harrow tankers of Sir Alan Cobham's Flight Refuelling Company, the Empire flying boats *Cabot* and *Caribou* were able to operate a transatlantic air-mail service in the summer of 1939.

460. The Mayo composite aircraft was another idea which used the fact that an aeroplane can fly with a greater load than it will lift off the ground. The heavily-loaded seaplane *Mercury* was carried into the air by the flying-boat mother-plane *Maia*, and launched in flight.

461-2. On 20th–21st July 1938 *Mercury* separated from *Maia* over Foynes, Ireland, and made the first non-stop flight between Britain and Montreal. This broke the record for the east-west route and was the first commercial crossing by a heavier-than-air machine, as *Mercury* carried 1,000 lb. of mail. In October 1938 the little seaplane set up the present seaplane distance record of 5,998 miles by flying non-stop from Dundee to the Orange River, South Africa. Its subsequent arrival at Capetown is shown above.

463. Biggest bomber built by 1937 was the 72-ton Douglas XB-19, one of two experimental long-range bombardment aeroplanes tested by the U.S. Air Corps. Four 2,200-h.p. engines gave it a speed of 204 m.p.h. Wing span was 212 ft. and it needed a crew of eleven. Used as a flying laboratory, it helped to make possible the giant inter-continental bombers of today.

464. Another, more hush-hush aircraft of 1937 was this Heinkel He.112 fighter, with an experimental 2,200-lb.-thrust liquid-fuel rocket-motor in its tail. Developed by the scientists who later produced the V.2 rocket, it led to the first rocket-fighter, the Heinkel He.176 of 1938, and the later, successful, Me.163.

465. First aircraft with a proper pressurised cabin was the Lockheed XC-35, built for high-altitude research. A high-flying, pressurised airliner – the Boeing Stratoliner – followed in 1939.

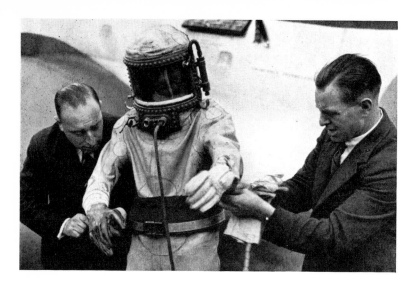

466–7. In the 1914–18 War the advantage in a dog-fight was held by the pilot who could dive on his enemy 'out of the sun'. Height was the key to victory in war. It is also the key to comfort in peace. An air liner that flies above the weather offers higher performance and a smoother ride. To probe the secrets of high flying, the Air Ministry ordered the Bristol Type 138 (*below*). In it, on 28th September 1936, Squad.-Ldr. Swain set up an aeroplane height record of 49,967 ft. Nine months later it was raised to 53,937 ft. by Flt.-Lt. M. J. Adam (*left*).

468. World height record of 72,395 ft. was set up on 11th November 1935 by Capts. Stevens and Anderson of the U.S. Air Corps in the balloon *Explorer II*. Although the gas-bag appears almost empty here, its gas expanded so much in the stratosphere that it filled out to a sphere of 3,700,000 cu. ft. – 46 times the size of a large sporting balloon.

469–70. Following a series of disasters, Britain, France and America abandoned airship development. Only Germany continued to operate across the Atlantic with the fine new Zeppelin *Hindenburg* (*left*). Flying time was 62 hours; but it was superbly comfortable. There was even a lightweight grand piano aboard. Then, on 6th May 1937, whilst being moored at Lakehurst, New Jersey, with terrifying suddenness the *Hindenburg* burst into a mass of flames. Thirty-five persons were killed, and world confidence in the big rigid airship died with them.

471. Public interest in aviation was bolstered by the air circus operated in the 1930's by Sir Alan Cobham and C. W. A. Scott. Between five-shilling joyrides, crowds all over the U.K. watched aerobatics, parachute drops, gliding, bombing with flour bags and other stunts. Popular item was when Geoffrey Tyson picked up a handkerchief on the wing-tip of his Tiger Moth (*left*).

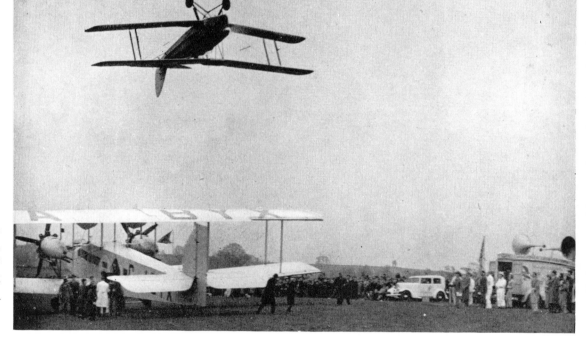

472. Famed for his very low inverted flying, Tyson crossed the Channel upside down in a Tiger Moth on the 25th anniversary of Blériot's pioneer Calais–Dover flight of 1909.

473. Ill-fated attempt to produce an aeroplane which anyone could build at home for £100 was Henri Mignet's *Pou-du-Ciel*, or 'Flying Flea'. It was banned after bad workmanship and unstable design killed several would-be airmen.

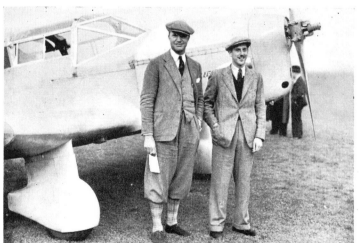

474. Less exciting than the 1934 Melbourne race, the England–Johannesburg contest in September 1936 was also won by C. W. A. Scott, in a Vega Gull. His companion was Giles Guthrie and they were the only crew to finish.

475. Records fell thick and fast in the 'thirties. Sensation of 1937 was the arrival in California of three Soviet airmen who had flown their ANT-25 monoplane non-stop 6,306 miles from Moscow, via the north pole. Flight took sixty-two hours.

476. Lone record flier was Alex Henshaw who won the King's Cup in a Percival Mew Gull at 236 m.p.h. in 1938, and, next year, set up new times for the London-Cape-Town-and-back flight.

477. Superb navigation enabled Howard Hughes and his four-man crew to fly around the world in 3 days 19 hours 14 minutes in the Lockheed 14 *New York World's Fair 1939*.

478. Britain regained the world long-distance record in 1938 when two R.A.F. Vickers Wellesley bombers flew non-stop from Ismailia in Egypt to Darwin, Australia, a distance of 7,158 miles. A third Wellesley ran short of fuel and landed at Timor Island.

479. The dreams of Leonardo da Vinci and countless others came true when the first successful helicopters were flown. In 1936, thirty years after becoming the first man to leave the ground in a rotating wing aircraft, Louis Breguet built this helicopter with contra-rotating rotors. It flew for more than an hour, covering twenty-seven miles.

480. First fully-controllable helicopter was the German Focke-Achgelis FW-61 (*right*). It set up records for duration (80 min.), speed (76 m.p.h.), and height (11,243 ft.), was flown inside the Deutschland Halle, Berlin, by Hanna Reitsch.

481. Even more important was the first flight of Igor Sikorsky's VS.300 (*below*) in September 1939. Returning to helicopter design after thirty years, during which he produced some of America's best passenger-carrying flying boats and amphibians, Sikorsky perfected this single-main-rotor aircraft and started the helicopter industry.

482. Deutsche Luft Hansa pioneered their transatlantic services with seaplanes launched from catapult ships. Biggest were the four-engined Blohm and Voss Ha.139 seaplanes *Nordmeer* and *Nordwind*, which made many mail-carrying flights across both the North and South Atlantic between 1937 and 1939.

483. Air survey photography for map-making is an important flying job. The Royal Canadian Air Force used these Vickers Vedette flying boats as camera-planes pre-war.

484. Super-streamlined air liner of 1938 was the all-wood De Havilland Albatross, which carried twenty-one passengers and had a top speed of 234 m.p.h. with four Gipsy-Twelve engines of only 510 h.p. each.

485. 'Flying for all' came to Britain in 1938 with the Government's Civil Air Guard scheme to create a reserve of men and women pilots behind the R.A.F. Here Plymouth members receive instruction on Hornet and Tiger Moths.

486.　The Thin Blue Line.　Pilots of No. 111 Squadron, Royal Air Force, with their Hurricanes, at Northolt in the last months of peace.

Air Power Supreme

Few people in Britain and France knew what to expect when their Governments declared war on Germany, on 3rd September 1939, two days after the German Army attacked Poland. They thought they would be bombed; but they were not. They thought the war would end quickly; but it did not – except in Poland, where the Nazi tactic of *blitzkrieg*, combined with a stab in the back from Russia, eliminated the Polish Army and Air Force in little more than a month.

In the west things remained quiet. American journalists called it the 'Phoney War'. But Polish airmen who escaped to the west with a fierce determination to fight on had no illusions that the calm would last. When the storm broke on Norway, Holland, Belgium and France they had seen it all before – the screaming *Stuka* dive-bombers that blasted a path for the tanks of the *Panzer* divisions.

The *Luftwaffe* showed convincingly what air power could achieve in support of ground forces and, in Norway, as a transport service for paratroops and airborne units. At Rotterdam, as at Warsaw, it demonstrated how bombers could tear the heart out of an undefended city in minutes. Next job was to pave the way for 'Operation Sea Lion', the invasion of Britain.

When the Battle of Britain started Air Chief Marshal Sir Hugh Dowding, A.O.C.-in-C. Fighter Command, had 704 serviceable aircraft, 620 of them Hurricanes and Spitfires – thanks in large measure to the efforts of the new Minister of Aircraft Production, Lord Beaverbrook. Opposing him were the 3,500 aircraft of *Luftflotte* 2 under Kesselring, *Luftflotte* 3 under Sperrle and *Luftflotte* 5 under Stumpff. Their fate, as smoking hulks in the harvest fields of Kent, Surrey and Sussex, is history.

The R.A.F. won because its leadership was sound; its aircraft superb; its pilots gallant beyond praise; its ground crews untiring; its raid-reporting organisation incredibly efficient; and its spirit unbeatable. It was an offensive, independent force, unshackled to the ground-borne strategies of armies and navies; and it won a great victory.

There were five more years of war; but after the Battle of Britain, even in the darkest days, defeat was unthinkable. The 'knights in shining armour' type of air warfare gave way to the grim monotony of wholesale destruction.

It all ended in the mushrooms of atomic dust over Hiroshima and Nagasaki, after Italy, Russia, Japan, the United States and half the world had entered battle. From a contraption of stick and canvas, the aeroplane had grown into a juggernaut against which armies, tanks and battleships were powerless, and which could destroy 71,000 humans in a single flash. Yet, in its unprecedented inhumanity, it held the key to future peace through fear – for although World War II was over, the possibility of war was as great as in 1939. But those who could start it knew that next time there would be no victor's crown, for there could be no joy in victory amid a radio-active wasteland.

When war started the Royal Air Force had a front-line force of 33 bomber squadrons; 19 coastal squadrons; and 35 fighter squadrons. Of these, a very large number were still equipped with obsolete biplanes. Even worse, ten of the bomber squadrons were sent to France as the Advanced Air Striking Force. In addition, 13 squadrons of Lysanders, Blenheims and Hurricanes formed the Air Component of the British Expeditionary Force in France.

487. Supermarine Spitfire. Most famous of all fighters, versions of the Spitfire remained in service throughout the war, and long after. More than 22,000 were built, including carrier-based Seafires.

488. Westland Lysander. This easily-recognised army co-operation aircraft was used also for night landings on the Continent to drop and collect agents and members of resistance forces.

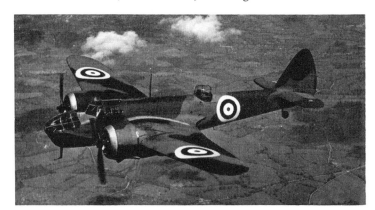

489. Bristol Blenheim. Standard day bomber and night fighter of the early war years, powered like the Lysanders with Mercury engines.

490. Avro Anson. Nicknamed 'Faithful Annie', this aircraft started the war as a coastal reconnaissance bomber, and then later became the R.A.F.'s standard crew trainer and light communications transport.

491. Armstrong Whitworth Whitley. One of Bomber Command's standard 'heavies' on the outbreak of war, Whitleys made most of the propaganda leaflet raids of 1939–40 and the first long-range attacks on Italy. Later used as paratroop transports and glider tugs.

492. Handley Page Hampden. Powered by two 980-h.p. Pegasus engines, this bomber was widely used for mine-laying and torpedo-attack duties. Its stalky tail-boom gave a good field of fire for the top and bottom rear-gunners.

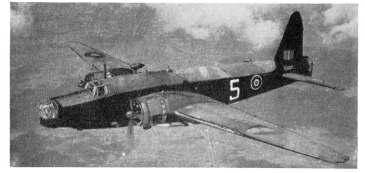

493. Vickers Wellington. Immortal as the 'Wimpy', this fine twin-engined bomber bore the brunt of Bomber Command's offensive until the four-motor 'heavies' were in service. It was the first to carry a 4,000-lb. 'block-buster' and was adapted for many duties.

494. Messerschmitt Me.109F/2. The *Luftwaffe's* counterpart to the Spitfire, which remained in service throughout the war.

The Luftwaffe, *unlike the Royal Air Force, was essentially an army support organisation. All its bombers, even the four-motor He.177 developed late in the war, had to be suitable for use as dive-bombers. Total first-line strength on 3rd September 1939 was 4,161 aircraft, compared with 1,911 R.A.F. aircraft. Comparable figures for 1st August 1940 were 4,549 and 2,913 respectively, plus 1,529 Italian aircraft.*

495. Focke-Wulf Fw.190. The *Luftwaffe's* standard fighter-bomber from 1941 to the end of the war. Very fast, with a top speed of 385 m.p.h., and heavily-armed, it was a formidable fighting machine.

496. Messerschmitt Me.110c. Designed as a fighter 'destroyer', the Me.110 proved too vulnerable in combat and was used mainly for fighter-bomber and night-fighter duties.

497. Junkers Ju.88. Most widely-used and most successful German bomber, the Ju.88 first flew in 1937, was developed during the war into a very efficient, radar-equipped night-fighter.

498. Dornier 215. Another of the *Luftwaffe's* standard bombers, the Do.215 carried 2,200 lb. of bombs for 900 miles. As in most German bombers, the crew of four were packed in the nose.

499. Heinkel He.111. Flown over England, and shot down in large numbers during the Battle of Britain, the He.111 was used also for torpedo attacks on Allied shipping. It was powered, like the Ju.88, with two Junkers Jumo engines of 1,100 – 1,300 h.p.

500. Fieseler Fi.156C Storch. One of Germany's most brilliant designs, the spindly Storch was able to land and take-off almost like a helicopter. Rommel and most other Army leaders used Storches as personal runabouts. Engine was a 240-h.p. As.10C.

First operation by the R.A.F. was a reconnaissance of German bases by a Blenheim of No. 139 Squadron on 3rd September 1939. Next day, ten Blenheims of Nos. 110 and 107 Squadrons made the first bombing raid, on German naval units in the Schillig Roads. Whitleys of Nos. 51 and 58 Squadrons dropped propaganda leaflets over Hamburg, Bremen and the Ruhr on the first night of war. The Luftwaffe, in return, began attacking British warships in the Firth of Forth. There was no bombing of land targets in Britain or Germany. This was the 'Phoney War'.

501. In Poland, Warsaw burned under the wings of departing German bombers. The campaign cost the *Luftwaffe* 600–700 aircraft and 1,000 airmen. The Polish air force lost 90 per cent of its aircraft and 70 per cent of its aircrews.

502. Stunned by Germany's new *blitzkrieg* tactics, infantry feared the dive-bomber Ju.87 *Stukas*, until they learned how vulnerable these aircraft were to fighter attack or well-aimed anti-aircraft fire. Screaming sirens added terror to the demoralizing suddenness of *Stuka* attacks. A single 1,100-lb. bomb was usually carried.

503. The *Entente Cordiale* in action. Battle day-bombers of the Advanced Air Striking Force, escorted by French Curtiss Hawk fighters. Although they achieved many successes, the 241 m.p.h., poorly-armed Battles stood little chance when attacked by *Luftwaffe* fighters. Altogether, the campaign in France in May and June 1940 cost the R.A.F. 959 aircraft. The *Luftwaffe* lost a total of 1,284.

504. Best French fighter was the 341 m.p.h. Dewoitine D.520, with 1,000-h.p. Hispano engine and armament of one cannon and two machine-guns. Few were delivered before the French collapse.

505. Amiot 370 bomber also would have served the French well had it been in service in quantity. In good aircraft, Free French refugee pilots later fought bravely with the R.A.F.

506.   Essential part of the *Luftwaffe's* duties was transport of troops, equipment and supplies to combat areas.   In Norway, it was a key to speedy victory.   Later, Crete became the first territory to fall to airborne assault, but at such high cost that Germany never again mounted a full-scale airborne operation.   Her superbly-trained paratroops were frittered away as infantry in Russia.

507.   Epic of the Norwegian campaign was the gallant fight by pilots of No. 263 Squadron, R.A.F., from the frozen surface of Lake Lesjaskog, near Aandalsnes. For four days they flew their Gladiator biplanes against vast formations of German bombers, until only one aircraft remained, for which there was no petrol. Re-equipped, No. 263 fought alongside the Hurricanes of No. 46 Squadron near Narvik, until evacuated by H.M.S. *Glorious.* Most of the pilots died when this carrier was sunk.

508.   After Norway, the *blitz* was turned on Holland, Belgium and France. Britain's army seemed lost; but while an armada of big and little ships snatched 340,000 men from under the guns of the *Panzer* divisions at Dunkirk, Hudsons of Coastal Command patrolled overhead. Behind the beaches, Hurricanes and Spitfires fought off the Stukas that could have made the rescue operation impossible.

509. Bombers over England. Incredibly, Hitler gave the R.A.F. two months to re-equip for battle before flinging the *Luftwaffe* into action. First, Channel convoys and ports were attacked; then the full might of three bomber fleets was turned against our fighter airfields. The Hurricanes and Spitfires fought against incredible odds; and the start of the night *blitz* on London in September was an admission that the *Luftwaffe* had been shot out of the daylight skies. Civilization had been saved by a thousand British boys.

510. Radar was the secret weapon which ensured victory. With the reports of the Royal Observer Corps, it guided R.A.F. fighters to the right place at the right moment, eliminating both surprise attack and time-wasting patrols. In this Operations Room, officers watch the progress of a raid on a large map.

511. The bell has clanged its alarm. Hurriedly one of the R.A.F.'s Polish pilots buckles on his parachute, while a mechanic warms the engine of his Spitfire. Death is five minutes away in the summer sky. Polish airmen shot down many of the 1,733 German aircraft destroyed in the Battle of Britain. R.A.F. losses totalled 915 aircraft.

512. Its fuselage torn by cannon-fire, an Me.109 forms strange harvest in a British cornfield. Hitler's march against England was misfiring.

513. When the *Luftwaffe* switched to night bombing in September 1940, its losses were small, for the R.A.F. had no efficient night fighters. Decoy airfields with dummy aircraft absorbed many bombs; and radio-countermeasures 'bent' the beams along which German bombers flew to their targets. But industry was sorely hit and, in eight months, 40,000 civilians were killed, another 46,000 injured and more than a million houses damaged for a loss of only 600 German aircraft – 1·5 per cent of the total sorties.

514. First real night fighter was the cannon-armed two-seater Beaufighter, which hunted its prey with radar 'eyes'.

515. Barrage balloons in key areas kept enemy bombers high, where shells from anti-aircraft guns were more effective. Kills improved from 20,000 rounds for each aircraft destroyed to less than 3,000 by February 1941. Later, radar-aimed guns and rockets achieved far better results.

516. Between 7th September and 13th November, 1940, the *Luftwaffe* dropped 13,000 tons of high explosive and 1,000,000 incendiary bombs on London. St. Paul's Cathedral, ringed with fire and rubble, stood firm; and so did the people of London. Under even heavier attack, the Germans later showed the same determination and bravery.

517. R.A.F. Bomber Command played its part in the Battle of Britain by destroying hundreds of the barges in which Hitler planned to ferry his armies across the Channel. Better bombers and bigger bombs enabled it to hit back hard at Germany; but before September 1941 only one in three aircraft arrived within five miles of its target. Accuracy came later, with radar navigation and bombing aids.

518. When Italy entered the war, the sole air defences of Malta, Britain's vital Mediterranean stronghold, comprised three Gladiator biplanes. Named *Faith*, *Hope* and *Charity*, they held off the Italian Air Force until Hurricanes arrived.

519. Malta was not secure until sufficient Spitfires arrived to deal with Italian and German massed raids. Serviced by Army and Air Force personnel, they provided cover for bombers and torpedo planes that sunk supply ships essential to Rommel's armies in Africa.

520. Major threat to British North African supply lines was removed on 11th November 1940, when 21 Swordfish biplanes from the carrier *Illustrious* made a night raid on the Italian fleet in Taranto Harbour. Reconnaissance next day showed that three battleships, a cruiser, two destroyers and two auxiliary vessels had been hit by torpedoes and bombs. Attack altered the balance of naval power in the Mediterranean at the cost of two Swordfish. This pre-war picture shows a Swordfish—affectionately known to its crews as 'Stringbags'—over the famous carrier, H.M.S. *Ark Royal*.

521. Through three years of fierce battling across North Africa, the Desert and North West African Air Forces never lost control of the air. Worst enemy was often the sand. Campaign cost Hitler and Mussolini 250,000 men, vast quantities of equipment and annihilation of the Italian fleet. The British and, later, the Americans learned to fight a war in which land, sea and air forces were closely integrated.

522. Italian Fiat fighter destroyed in Cyrenaica, 1940, when two British divisions and 200 aircraft routed nine Italian divisions and 400 aircraft in two months.

523. Hurricane IID fighters, with 40-mm. guns under their wings, destroyed many German tanks during the final campaign from El Alamein to Tunis, October 1942–May 1943. Guns were soon superseded by more deadly, accurate rockets.

524. Seldom in the headlines, aircraft of R.A.F. Coastal Command and from escort carriers of the Allied navies protected countless convoys, attacked and sank a high proportion of the 722 enemy submarines destroyed during the 5½ year Battle of the Atlantic, the vital lifeline between Britain and America. Sunderland flying boats were called 'Flying Porcupines' by respectful German fighter pilots, because of their defensive armament of eight machine-guns.

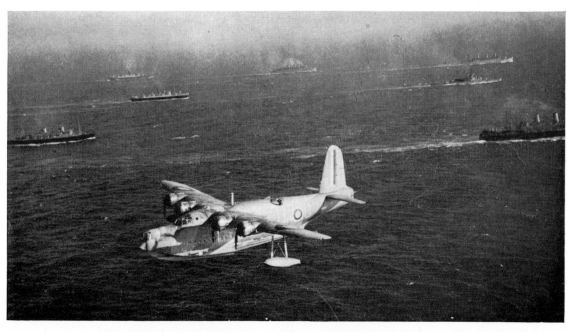

525. Conceived in 1936, the R.A.F.'s giant four-motor night bombers, with the U.S.A.A.F.'s B-17 and B-24 day bombers, waged a merciless 24-hour bomber offensive against Hitler's 'Fortress Europe'. First in action in February 1941, the Short Stirling carried 7 tons of bombs for 590 miles, was armed with eight machine-guns.

526. Finest bomber of its day, the Avro Lancaster spearheaded Bomber Command's offensive, and was the only aircraft able to carry the 22,000-lb. Grand Slam bomb. It was also used for the famous 'Dam-busting' raid by No. 617 Squadron, led by Guy Gibson.

527. Aircraft which, with the Lancaster, bore the burden of the R.A.F.'s assault on Europe in the last years of war was the Handley Page Halifax. With a top speed of 270 m.p.h., it could carry 13,000 lb. of bombs for 850 miles.

528. When the 'heavies' were not over Berlin, the city's defences were kept busy by nimble Mosquitoes. Faster than most German fighters, and with a wooden airframe that produced only feeble flickers on enemy radar screens, the Mosquito was more than just a nuisance, with its 4,000-lb. 'block-buster' bomb-load. Night fighter and reconnaissance versions also achieved great success. Hoping to produce an equally effective high-speed bomber, Hitler delayed production of the Me.262 jet-fighter for a year while it was converted into a fighter-bomber. Had he not done so, the 262 might have brought the U.S. daylight bomber offensive to a standstill in 1943–4.

529. B-17 Fortresses of the 381st Bomb Group, U.S. 8th Air Force, weave their vapour trails high over France as they drone towards Wilhelmshaven, 3rd February 1944. Often more than 700 bombers flew in close formation on a single raid, escorted by hundreds of fighters. By the end of the war 31 German cities had 500 acres or more destroyed. Berlin alone lost 6,437 acres – ten times as much as London. 305,000 Germans were killed. 7½ million made homeless. Secondary duty of the Fortresses and their escort was to destroy the German Air Force in the air and on the ground.

530. Lockheed P.38 Lightnings were used for bomber escort and photo-reconnaissance. In three weeks before and after the Allied landings in France, 1944, they took three million photographs of the invasion coastline.

531. Finest long-range escort fighter was the North American P-51 Mustang. Produced originally to R.A.F. specification, it could escort bombers all the way to Berlin and back. Maximum speed was 450 m.p.h.

532. Typical of the new types developed by the Soviet aircraft industry since the Spanish and Finnish wars was the PE-2 light bomber. Pilots of the R.A.F. wing sent to Russia in 1941 found it faster than their Hurricane fighters.

533. Like the *Luftwaffe*, the Soviet Air Force was intended mainly to support operations by the Red Army and had few strategic bombers. MiG-3's were among its best fighters. A 1,200 h.p. AM-35A engine gave them a speed of 360 m.p.h.

534. Greatest air effort in history preceded the Allied invasion of Europe, 6th June 1944. In 200,000 sorties 200,000 tons of bombs were dropped, the enemy's railways were blasted beyond immediate repair, his radar system disrupted and the forthcoming battlefield isolated by destroying all the Seine bridges between Paris and the sea. On British airfields, hundreds of gliders waited to add their human cargoes to those who went by sea.

535. Terror of the German infantry and *Panzer* divisions in France was the rocket-firing Hawker Typhoon fighter-bomber.

536. With complete control of the air, the R.A.F. could even spare Spitfires to carry tanks of beer for the troops.

537. Day and night the air offensive continued on and behind the battlefield. Fuel and the *Luftwaffe* were the main targets, together with the mushrooming 'V' weapon sites on the Channel coast. Here Marauders of the U.S. Army Air Force raid an enemy airfield.

538. Allied airborne assault on the bridges at Arnhem, Nijmegen and Grave was an attempt to outflank the Siegfried defence line and end the war quickly. Later use of airborne forces to speed the Rhine crossing at Wesel was completely successful.

539. World's first jet-rotor helicopter – the Doblhoff – was just one of the many advanced aircraft developed by the enemy.

540. For attacks on heavily-protected targets, the *Luftwaffe* filled the noses of Ju.88's with explosive and launched them as glider-bombs from F.W.190 fighters.

541. Fastest aircraft of its day was the 560 m.p.h. Messerschmitt Me.163 rocket-fighter. With enough fuel for only twelve minutes, its endurance could be extended by switching off the rocket and gliding. Armament was two 30-mm. cannons.

542. One of Germany's best night fighters was the Ju.388J, with two Jumo 222E engines, an extremely heavy armament of six cannon and extensive radar. Top speed was 414 m.p.h. at 37,700 ft.

543. First of the Wellsian reprisal weapons with which Hitler hoped to win the war at the eleventh hour was the jet-powered V.1 flying bomb. Extremely ingenious, it carried 1,870 lb. of explosive 150 miles at 390 m.p.h. Of 7,547 launched against Britain, fighters destroyed 1,847, anti-aircraft guns 1,866, balloon cables 232 and the Royal Navy 12. Those that got through killed 6,139 people.

544. (*Right*) Even more advanced was the V.2 liquid-fuel war rocket, the first of which hit London on 8th September 1944. To carry a ton of explosive 200 miles, it reached a speed of about 3,600 m.p.h. and a height of 60 miles before starting its dive into the target. The 1,115 V.2's fired against England killed 2,855 people.

545–6. War in the Far East started when Japanese carrier-borne aircraft attacked the U.S. naval base at Pearl Harbour, Hawaii, on 7th December 1941. Four battleships were sunk, many other warships damaged, giving Japan command of the seas. Nearby U.S. Air Force stations were also heavily attacked, causing destruction or damage of 150 aircraft.

547. Shock for Allied pilots was the fast, highly manœuvrable Jap Zero fighter, which took heavy toll of obsolete British and American aircraft. This captured Zero carries U.S. markings.

548. Support first for the Chinese and then for Allied armies in Burma came from Gen. Claire Chennault's American Volunteer Group, who claimed destruction of 280 Jap aircraft.

549. Value of air supply was proved during the Burma campaign of 1945, when 17 Dakota squadrons, unaided, kept an army of 356,000 troops in action against the retreating Japanese.

550. Japan's most effective weapons were the *Kamikaze* suicide bombers. In ten months *Kamikazes* accounted for forty-eight per cent of all U.S. warships damaged and twenty-one per cent of those sunk in the whole 44-month Pacific War.

551. A British carrier is hit by the death-dive of a *Kamikaze* pilot, off the Sakishima Islands. Because of their armoured decks, British carriers were in action within two hours of such attacks. Wooden-decked U.S. carriers suffered much more severely. Pilots of *Kamikazes* were often high-ranking officers from Japan's best families, believing, through their religion, that self-sacrifice earned them a place in its divine hierarchy.

552. (*Above*) Object of the grim island-hopping campaign across the Pacific was to capture bases from which U.S. bombers could hammer the Japanese homeland. From the Marianas, B-29 Superfortresses flew day after day in their hundreds, working to a systematic plan which burned the heart out of 66 major cities.

553. (*Below*) Japan had been bombed almost to submission when, on 6th August 1945, an atomic bomb was loaded on to the B-29 *Enola Gay* and flown to Hiroshima by Col. Paul Tibbets (*below, right*). By evening the city and 71,379 of its people no longer existed.

554. Three days later, while the inner council of the Japanese government discussed surrender terms in Tokyo, a blinding flash devastated Nagasaki and once more the characteristic mushroom cloud of death billowed up to 20,000 ft. On 15th August Japan surrendered and World War II had ended.

The New Pioneer Age

WORLD War II accelerated aviation progress to an unprecedented degree. Before it ended combat aircraft were flying into action at speeds far higher than the pre-war record of 469 m.p.h. The Atlantic was being crossed as mere routine by ordinary Service pilots as they swarmed to Britain for the final assault on Hitler's 'Fortress Europe'. The ashes of burned-out, devastated cities, the twisted remains of tanks and guns, the rusting hulks of countless ships that would never sail again, an aching emptiness in the hearts of parents, widows and orphans all over the world, all bore tragic witness of the supreme power of the aeroplane in every sphere of war. And the V.2 rocket lifted the nightmare of push-button warfare and the dream of space-flight out of the pages of science fiction into the fear-filled skies over Europe.

Captured enemy records showed that the Germans had made incredible progress in every sphere of aviation. Their rocket fighters and designs for very fast swept-wing jet-planes were far more advanced than anything the Allies had. Their research in aerodynamics, rocket engines, guided missiles, aviation medicine and other subjects was so thorough and startling that it has formed the basis for most post-war military aviation research in Britain, America and Russia.

At first, when peace returned, it was hoped that the United Nations would indeed prove to be united. Aviation quickly showed its ability to bring relief, comfort and hope to a world that badly needed all three. Food was rained down to the starving people of the Netherlands, instead of bombs. In one month alone the Dakotas, Stirlings and Halifaxes of Nos. 38 and 46 Groups, R.A.F., flew home to England 27,277 British and American prisoners-of-war. And, in the strength and speed of aviation's new wings, people in every country saw hope of commerce and travel that would make their lives more full and more enjoyable in the peaceful years ahead.

The legacy of war included a network of fine large airfields in almost every land, and a new generation of superb transport aircraft, designed to carry troops and equipment, but easily adapted for civilian passengers and cargo. The two sounded the death knell of the civil flying boat, for no major international airline could continue paying for water bases which they alone used, while their competitors enjoyed the privileges of state-subsidised land aerodromes. So although B.O.A.C., Air France and a handful of other operators ran flying-boat services for a few years, they gradually converted to all-landplane fleets.

This gave U.S. aircraft companies a tremendous advantage; because it had been agreed during the war that America should build all transport aircraft needed by the R.A.F. and U.S.A.A.F., leaving Britain free to concentrate on warplane production. In 1946 airlines had the choice of buying American Constellations, Skymasters, DC-6's, Stratocruisers and Convair-Liners, or of trying to make do with converted bombers and 'interim' aircraft like the York and Viking, which were based on bomber designs. Most, like B.O.A.C., ordered new U.S. machines for their 'prestige' routes, and worked the others with makeshift types.

Behind the scenes, British designers planned to regain their lost leadership by by-passing completely the stage of air-liner development represented by the U.S. aircraft, and staking everything on revolutionary new high-performance air-liners with turbojet and propeller-turbine engines. One result was the Comet; the other the Britannia and Viscount, which earned Britain much larger orders than any previous airliner in flying history. Even highly nationalist U.S. airlines were forced to buy the Viscount, to avoid being outflown in the new age of faster, more comfortable, economical air travel that it made possible.

Key to Britain's success was the excellence of her jet and propeller-turbine engines, which have since been chosen to power many of the finest and fastest aircraft built in America, France, Sweden and even Russia, until Soviet designers learned new skills. Unfortunately, many are still being fitted in warplanes; for VE-Day and VJ-Day ended one war only to start a 'cold war' between East and West.

Fear of the consequences of a new global war, waged with atomic and hydrogen bombs, has so far maintained an uneasy peace, punctuated with bitter local fighting in Korea, Malaya, Vietnam and other danger spots. So long as America and Russia continue to maintain their vast bomber and missile forces, this 'peace through fear' will continue.

Certainly air power averted a major conflict in 1948–9, when Russia blockaded Berlin, and America and Britain kept a city of $2\frac{1}{4}$ million people alive and at work by air supply alone. Such an achievement had been termed impossible, particularly through the winter months. The Berlin Air Lift proved it possible and saved the lives of untold millions.

Today, there seems no limit to aviation progress. The once-dreaded 'sound-barrier' proved but a hurdle that could be overcome by science and courage; and now the speed of sound is merely a yardstick by which we measure performance. Already man has flown at 4,534 m.p.h., and climbed above Earth's atmosphere to the fringe of space. New metals, new engines, new fuels, new shapes will bring still more spectacular flights, for continued research, however costly, holds the key to survival in the struggle for mastery of the air.

Not all the results are for war. Already more than 500 million people a year travel the air routes of the world for trade and pleasure. Their safety is assured by miracles of radio and radar engineering that will guide an air-liner automatically over the longest routes, to a safe landing in any weather.

Even more fantastic developments are on the way, for we are at the 'Wright Brothers' stage of a completely new era of pioneering in supersonic travel, quieter aero-engines and methods of vertical take-off that may well dispense in time with complex, expensive runways, and permit safe, convenient air travel from near the heart of our cities to the four corners of the world. Yet even that will not be the end, for other worlds beckon us across the dark emptiness of interplanetary space and near relatives of the fearful rocket weapons forged for man's destruction have already begun to carry him far beyond Earth's bounds on the greatest adventures of all time.

555. Greatest technical advance of World War II was the development of jet-propelled warplanes. Jet-engines for aircraft had been suggested in the old pioneer days; but serious work awaited production of metals that would withstand the intense heat and stresses involved. First patents were taken out in England by Frank Whittle in 1930, followed five years later by Hans von Ohain's patents in Germany. After many disappointments Whittle's Power Jets company gained in 1939 a contract for jet-engines for flight testing in an airframe to be built by the Gloster company. Meanwhile, Ohain and Dr. Ernst Heinkel had built a 1,100 lb. thrust jet-engine known as the He.S.3B and fitted it in the He.178 (left). On 27th August 1939 this became the first jet-propelled aeroplane to fly.

556–7. Italy's contribution to early jet pioneering was the Caproni-Campini monoplane. Less advanced than the Whittle and Ohain jets, the compressor of its engine was driven by an ordinary piston-engine. Performance was rather disappointing, with a top speed of only 205 m.p.h., and the aircraft was abandoned in 1942, after making a number of much-publicized flights.

558. For his work in developing practical jet-engines Frank Whittle received a knighthood and tax-free award of £100,000 post-war. Samples of his engines, sent to America in 1941, powered the first U.S. jet aircraft and gave a start to the U.S. turbojet industry.

559. First British jet-plane to fly, on 15th May 1941, was the Gloster E.28/39, powered by an 860 lb. thrust Whittle W-1 turbojet. The second prototype, with a more powerful engine, achieved 466 m.p.h. and a height of 42,000 ft.

560. Delivery of the Messerschmitt Me.262 twin-jet fighter was delayed for a year, while it was converted for bomb-carrying, by Hitler's orders. If this had not happened, the 527-m.p.h. fighter, with its heavy armament of 30-mm. guns and rockets, might have stopped the U.S. daylight bomber offensive in 1944.

561. America's first jet-plane was the Bell XP-59A Airacomet, flown on 1st October 1942. Power units were two I-16 turbojets, developed by General Electric from the Whittle W-1X, and the aircraft had a top speed of 413 m.p.h. Altogether fifty were built and used for pilot training.

562. Although closely resembling the Me.262, the Japanese Kikka naval attack fighter was designed by the Nakajima company and had two 1,047 lb. thrust Ne-20 engines. The prototype, built on a farm as most aircraft factories had been bombed, flew on the day after the first atomic bomb hit Hiroshima.

563. Only Allied jet used in action in World War II was the Meteor, which was used by No. 616 Squadron, R.A.F., to destroy V.1 flying bombs, and then taken to the Continent. Soon after the war the public was given a glimpse of the capabilities of jet-propelled aircraft when a Meteor 4, piloted by Group Capt. Wilson, set up a World Speed Record of 606·38 m.p.h., which exceeded the old record by no less than 137 m.p.h. Later, another Meteor 4, piloted by Group Capt. Donaldson, raised the record to 615·81 m.p.h.

564. First flown in 1944 with a de Havilland Goblin turbojet, and later re-engined with a General Electric J33, the Lockheed F-80 Shooting Star was America's first operational jet-fighter. A specially hotted-up prototype raised the speed record to 623.74 m.p.h. in 1947.

565. The speed record fell twice more in 1947, in each case to the Douglas Skystreak research plane. Pilot on the second attempt was Major Marion Carl of the U.S. Marine Corps, who averaged 650·92 m.p.h. in two runs over a 3-km. course.

566. Most spectacular event of the year, on 14th October 1947, was the first faster-than-sound flight by the rocket-powered Bell X-1 research aircraft, after it had been carried to 30,000 ft. under a Superfortress mother-plane. British firms had been forbidden to build piloted supersonic machines, as attempts to crash the 'sound barrier' were considered too dangerous, following a series of fatal accidents to high-speed aeroplanes.

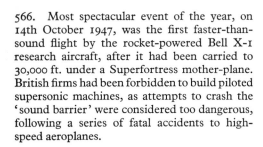

567. Pilot on the first supersonic flight was Major Charles 'Chuck' Yeager, U.S.A.F.

568. Bell X-1 in flight. A later version, designated X-1A, was flown at 1,650 m.p.h. by Yeager, and reached a height of 90,000 ft. Power plant was a four-barrelled rocket-motor, giving 6,000 lb. thrust.

569. Although production was cut back heavily after the war, few companies found themselves in difficulties. Necessity to re-equip with jet-planes kept the military assembly lines busy. In America, firms like Convair found a ready market for their modern, high-performance transports. The twin-engined Convair-Liner 240 became the standard medium-range air liner of many U.S. and European airlines, carrying forty passengers for up to 1,800 miles at 270 m.p.h.

570. World long-distance record was broken in 1946 by the U.S. Navy Lockheed Neptune *Truculent Turtle*, which flew non-stop 11,229 miles from Perth, Australia, to Columbus, Ohio.

571. A different kind of record was set up by the U.S.A.F.'s B-50 Superfortress *Lucky Lady II*, which encircled the world non-stop in 1949, by refuelling four times from Superfortress flying tankers.

572. Possibilities of air freighting were demonstrated when five jeeps were flown from Detroit to Los Angeles in 10 hours aboard the big Convair Model 39 cargo plane. Weighing 2,400 lb. each, the jeeps represented the first commercial air shipment of heavy vehicles in the United States. A full cargo of fruit and vegetables made up the return load.

573. With the pre-war air terminal at Croydon no longer suitable for major international airline operations, the partially-built R.A.F. station at Heath Row in Middlesex was taken over as the future London Airport. Early photographs show its original R.A.F. runway pattern.

574. When the first passenger services flew in to London Airport in January 1946 large brown tents formed the passenger-handling buildings. An American traveller said: 'Gee, where are the elephants?'

575. First control tower was this modest, square red-brick affair which gave good service until the fine new 127-ft.-high tower was opened in 1955.

576. First take-off from the new airport, on 1st January 1946, was by the Lancastrian *Star Light* of British South American Airways, on the Corporation's initial survey flight across the South Atlantic. Like *Star Dust* (right), *Star Light* was a converted Lancaster bomber, with accommodation for thirteen passengers. B.S.A.A. were later amalgamated with B.O.A.C., which also used Lancastrians to bring Australia within sixty-three hours of Britain by scheduled passenger service.

577. Aircraft with which British European Airways built up their reputation for safety and comfort was the Vickers Viking – a development of the wartime Wellington bomber. Seating up to thirty-six passengers, Vikings carried about $2\frac{3}{4}$ million persons and flew a total of $65\frac{1}{2}$ million miles in their eight years of service with the Corporation.

578. Like Australia's famous Royal Flying Doctor Service, B.E.A.'s Scottish Air Ambulance Unit brings speedy medical care to isolated communities. For many years the unit was equipped with Rapide biplanes.

579. Another veteran which saw worldwide service after the war was the DC-3 Dakota, with seats for 21–36 passengers. Douglas had produced 10,123 in four years as the standard troop and supply transports of the wartime Allied forces.

580. One of the brightest ideas in early post-war civil aviation was the England-France air ferry opened in July 1948 by Silver City Airways. Bristol Superfreighters and Freighters, each carrying up to three cars and twelve passengers, made the crossing in twenty minutes. To cater for rapidly-growing traffic, Silver City built their own airport at Ferryfield, Dungeness, from which ferry planes landed and took off at $3\frac{1}{2}$-minute intervals on peak days. With no suitable replacement for the Superfreighter, and the advent of the Hovercraft, the air ferry eventually declined.

581. Although based on the Superfortress atom-bomber, Boeing's Stratocruiser air liner was used on the transatlantic luxury services of B.O.A.C. and Pan American World Airways. Seating up to 100 passengers, the giant aircraft was complete with a lower-deck cocktail lounge, reached by spiral staircase from the main cabin.

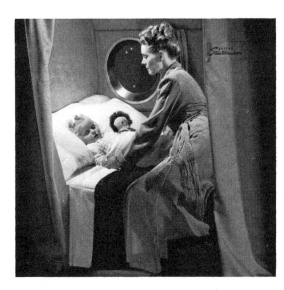

582. Planned by a world-famous designer, the interior of K.L.M.'s Lockheed Super Constellations reflected the standard of comfort and good taste offered by air liners of the 1950's.

583. Flying high, above the bad weather, passengers could sleep peacefully as their air liners whisked them at 300 m.p.h. above oceans and continents.

584. H.M. the Queen – then Princess Elizabeth – and the Duke of Edinburgh leave the B.O.A.C. Stratocruiser *Canopus* at Montreal for the start of their tour of Canada and visit to Washington.

585. Like King George VI, the Duke of Edinburgh is a qualified pilot and keen air traveller. Other royal pilots include the King of Jordan, the Shah of Persia and Prince Bernhardt of the Netherlands.

586. Britain's pace-setting in the air was born in the drawing offices, workshops and test houses of her engine manufacturers. Here engineers watch the trials of a Dart propeller-turbine in a test cell at the Rolls-Royce works. Unrivalled for power and reliability, British jet-engines were soon being built in almost every foreign country with an aircraft industry.

587. Pride of B.E.A., and airlines in every continent from America to Australia, were their fleets of Viscount air liners, powered by four Dart propeller-turbines. One of the few aircraft to make money from the start of its service life, the Viscount was also the first British air liner ordered for regular service inside the United States. Stage-coach ceremony marked its introduction into B.E.A. service; while the helicopter symbolised future city centre airbus services.

588. Departure of the first passenger-carrying service by Comet jet-liner from London Airport to Johannesburg, 1952. Although B.O.A.C. later paid a high price for its pioneering, all major airlines were to switch to high-speed luxury jet-flight during the following decade, and a later version of the Comet was to fly the first transatlantic jet services, for B.O.A.C., in 1958.

589–91. When Russia closed all surface routes into West Berlin in the summer of 1948, Britain and America took the bold decision to fly in all the food and supplies needed by the city's 2¼ million people. Day and night, a vast armada of American and British transport aircraft flew along narrow air corridors into the airports of Tempelhof and Gatow at intervals of two to five minutes, depending on the weather. Berlin stayed not only alive but at work, and in May 1949 the Russians lifted the blockade. Even then, the aerial life-lines were kept going until October 1949, to build up the city's reserves. In the total fifteen-month period the U.S. and British air forces, with the help of British civil charter firms, flew in 2,326,205 tons of supplies in 277,728 sorties, and proved that air power could prevent as well as win wars.

592. Night scene at Tempelhof, 1949. Dakotas were the mainstay of the Air Lift in the early weeks. Later, the bulk of the work was done by U.S. Skymasters and R.A.F. Yorks. Most impressive operations were made by flying boats of R.A.F. Coastal Command and Aquila Airways, which alighted on the Havelsee, to the great surprise of Berliners.

593–5. Petrol and oil were flown into Berlin by British independent airlines, including Airflight, whose Tudors carried ten tons of fuel at a time. The company's managing director, the wartime Pathfinder bomber chief, Air Vice-Marshal D. C. T. Bennett, flew many of the sorties himself (*above left*). Biggest aircraft used was the Douglas C-74 Globemaster (*above right*), which had a twenty-two-ton payload. It proved that a few very large aircraft would have been more efficient than the big fleet of Skymasters and Yorks; but its heavy weight broke up the runways and taxi-tracks at Tempelhof.

Victory in the cold war was not achieved without cost. Operations had to be flown in conditions that would have grounded the airlines, and only superb flying and traffic control made the Air Lift possible at all. Altogether fifty-one airmen died in seventeen serious accidents, and on the left Berliners watch silently as the wreckage of a Dakota is carried through their city.

596. Communism struck again on 25th June 1950, in Korea. In the van of United Nations forces which rushed to help the South Koreans were warships of the Royal Navy. Throughout the three-year campaign aircraft from British carriers provided support for the land forces.

597. At first there was little opposition to Allied air power. Pilots of the U.S. 68th All Weather Fighter Interceptor Squadron, based in Japan, saw nothing strange in flying into battle under the eyes of their family, knowing they would be home for tea. Later, when China entered the war, air combat became more grim.

598. Unsung heroes of the Korean War were pilots of the slow T-6 'Mosquito' spotter planes of the U.S.A.F., whose job was to find, and mark with smoke bombs and rockets, targets for United Nations fighters and bombers.

599. The helicopter became a fully-fledged weapon of war in Korea. As a front-line transport, it was able to carry squads of troops and their equipment speedily to almost inaccessible mountain positions. Rescue Helicopters evacuated 22,000 wounded, often under fire.

600. Boeing B-29 Superfortress bombers wrought such havoc in North Korea that, towards the end of the war, there were no worthwhile targets left to bomb. Main Chinese bases, and the airfields from which their MiG-15 jet fighters flew, were over the Yalu River in neutral Manchuria.

601. Air supply and paratroop drops played an important part in the fighting. Here a C-119 transport of the U.S. Far East Air Force's Combat Cargo Command drops rations and fuel to troops on the snow-covered battlefield.

602. Finest fighters of the Korean War were the U.S.A.F.'s F-86 Sabres, which destroyed 801 Communist MiG-15's. Only fifty-eight Sabres were lost in air combat.

603. Powered by a Soviet copy of the Rolls-Royce Nene, Russia's vaunted MiG-15 showed itself fast, manœuvrable and heavily armed; but its pilots were less skilled than those of the United Nations, and it lacked battle-winning refinements like a radar gun-sight.

604. Canadian-built de Havilland Beaver light transports served with U.S. Army Field Forces in Korea, after winning a design contest against strong competition from U.S. manufacturers. They proved so successful that America later ordered also the larger de Havilland Otter.

M

605. The war in Korea, trouble in Indo-China, Kenya and Malaya, and the continued "cold war" implied that the only hope of safety and peace lay in a high state of military preparedness. Aircraft factories all over the world became busier than at any time since the war. These Thunderjet fighter-bombers, on the assembly line in Republic's 1,600,000 sq. ft. factory on Long Island, New York, were destined to modernise the air forces of France, Holland, Greece, Turkey and other NATO countries. They were followed in production by faster, swept-wing F-84F Thunderstreaks, capable of carrying tactical atomic bombs.

606. Greatest need was to build up a powerful deterrent to aggression, and this demanded an increase in the range and speed of bomber forces, to permit attacks on distant targets and to elude defending jet-fighters. The Convair GRB-36 was a revival of the old flying aircraft-carrier idea, combining the 10,000-mile range of the B-36 bomber with the supersonic speed of a Thunderstreak fighter-bomber or Thunderflash photo-reconnaissance aircraft. The fighter was intended to be carried under the bomber until within easy range of the target, when it would be lowered on a trapeze and launched on its mission. Later it would be retrieved and flown back to base. In this way, the slower, more vulnerable B-36 need never have flown within range of the target's defences.

607. By 1958, the B-36 had been superseded in the U.S.A.F.'s Strategic Air Command by the huge 200-ton eight-jet Boeing B-52 Strato-fortress, here seen being refuelled in flight by a four-jet KC-135 Stratotanker. Flight refuelling has been adopted on a large scale by the U.S.A.F., U.S. Navy and R.A.F. Bomber Command. Its possibilities were demonstrated dramatically in January 1957, when three B-52's flew around the world non-stop, refuelling in mid-air several times *en route*. They covered 24,325 miles at an average speed of 530 m.p.h. and made a dummy bombing attack at the half-way mark.

608. To keep pace with the ever-increasing speed and height of jet-bombers, interceptor fighters have become semi-automatic. The pilot is guided by ground control until he nears his target; then he sits back and lets radar in the aircraft's nose fly it by passing signals to the automatic pilot. Following every moment of the enemy until it is within range, the radar fires the fighter's armament automatically, after which the pilot resumes control and flies home to re-arm. Typical is the Convair F-106A Delta Dart, which carries two Genie nuclear-warhead missiles and a battery of Falcon homing weapons in its fuselage weapon-bay. A hit from any one would destroy the biggest bomber ever built.

609. As weights and landing speeds increased, fighters like this North American F-100 Super Sabre had to be fitted with a tail parachute to slow them after touchdown. Able to fly faster than sound in level flight, an F-100 set up the first supersonic World Speed Record of 822.135 m.p.h. in 1955.

610. More missile than aeroplane, the Lockheed F-104A Starfighter has a 16,000 lb. thrust J79 turbojet and tiny wings, each of which spans only 7½ ft. from root to tip. Within a period of nine days in May 1958 Starfighters set up a World height record of 91,249 ft. and a World speed record of 1,404.19 m.p.h.

611. First U.S.A.F. supersonic strategic bomber was the Convair B-58 Hustler, which could fly at 1,380 m.p.h. Powered by four J79 turbojets, it carried under its fuselage a pod housing an atomic weapon and extra fuel.

612. Sea power has become of vital importance in an age when land bases are vulnerable to attack by atom-bombers and rockets. Aircraft carriers can be used as mobile bases for such bombers. Their efficiency has been improved tremendously by new British development such as the steam catapult and the angled flight deck, first fitted to the U.S.S. *Antietam* (above). The angled deck enables aircraft to be flow off or landed on the rear deck, while others are parked on the fore-deck, or being catapulted off.

613. The U.S. Navy has also studied the possibility of using self-contained Seaplane Striking Forces, able to operate in enemy waters in wartime. Fighter protection for such Forces might be given by aircraft like the Convair Sea Dart, first warplane with a hydro-ski undercarriage to permit rough water take-off and landing.

614. The Convair Tradewind flying boat was evaluated as a possible transport for supplies and servicing crews of Seaplane Striking Forces. Powered by four 5,500-h.p. turboprops, this graceful craft could carry 103 troops or 24 tons of cargo for 4,500 miles, and discharge them through bow loading doors, like a tank-landing ship.

615. The 600-m.p.h. Martin SeaMaster was envisaged as the basis of the Striking Forces. Most advanced flying boat ever built, it had four large turbojets and was intended for mine-laying and photo-reconnaissance. It proved that a flying boat of its time could be as fast and efficient as a landplane.

616. Value of carrier bases was proved again during the Suez operation of November 1956. These Whirlwind helicopters of the Royal Navy flew men of No. 45 Royal Marine Commando into action from H.M.S. *Theseus*.

617. Heavily-armed with rockets and cannons, Hawker Sea Hawk fighters were catapulted from H.M.S. *Eagle* to provide close support for the Anglo-French ground forces at Port Said.

618. Greater potential threat than even the aircraft-carrier is the missile-carrying submarine, able to creep up undetected to an enemy coastline, launch its atomic missiles and disappear again. The U.S.S. *Tunny* carried two 600 m.p.h. Regulus "flying bombs" in a deck-hangar. It was followed by the first of 41 U.S. Navy Polaris submarines, each able to fire 16 giant atomic rockets without having to surface.

619–20. Daring scheme adopted post-war by the R.A.F. was to start all its pupils on the 550-h.p. Hunting Provost basic trainer (*left*), instead of on slower, less complex primary trainers. Unsuitable pupils were weeded out more quickly, and good ones passed straight from the Provost on to Vampire jet-powered advanced trainers (*right*). The piston-engined Provost was later replaced by Jet Provosts, which are even more fast and powerful, but avoid the problem of having to unlearn piston-engined techniques when passing to jet advanced trainers.

621. In February 1957, the British Government announced a reorganisation of its defence forces that was described as the most revolutionary in military history. No strategic bombers were to be ordered beyond those already in production and no fighter beyond the English Electric Lightning then about to enter production. Instead, major efforts and expenditure were to be devoted to the perfection of guided missiles for defence and attack. Many experts believed the abandoning of new piloted aircraft to be premature, and so it proved.

Standard R.A.F. day-fighter at that period was the Hawker Hunter F.6 (left), armed with four powerful 30 mm. cannon. Several countries still operate fighter-bomber versions of this aircraft in the 'seventies.

622. One of the last big, four-engined strategic bombers built for the R.A.F. was the Handley Page Victor (centre) with crescent-shape wings which combined the advantages of both swept and straight wings. It flew just below the speed of sound at well over 50,000 feet, carrying nuclear weapons. When its task was done, it was converted for flight refuelling tanker duties.

623. First British jet-bomber, the English Electric Canberra (bottom left) was also built in America for the U.S.A.F. This particular machine, with a Napier Scorpion experimental rocket-engine in its bomb-bay, set up a World Altitude Record of 70,309 ft. in 1957.

624. With limited 'local' wars more likely than major war in an atomic age, the mobility of ground forces has assumed great importance. For carrying up to 70 paratroops or 22 tons of freight, the R.A.F. used the giant Blackburn Beverley in the 'sixties'.

625. Another of the R.A.F.'s final generation of big four-jet nuclear bombers was the delta-wing Avro Vulcan. A few squadrons have survived into the 'seventies, including one equipped for long-range photo-reconnaissance.

626. Latest British interceptor ordered for the Royal Air Force, the English Electric Lightning has two Avon turbojets staggered one above the other in its massive fuselage. It has a top speed approaching 1,500 m.p.h. Armament comprises two 30 mm. cannon and two Firestreak guided missiles which "home" automatically on the hot engines of an enemy aircraft.

627. Private flying became so costly post-war that few people could afford their own lightplanes at first. But companies began to buy them as speedy transports for their executives, and they were adapted for duties such as crop-spraying to kill insect and weed pests.

628. Helicopters are used extensively for crop spraying. This Hiller 360 helped to destroy cotton jassid insects in the Sudan.

629. All kinds of animals have been carried by air since the war. They have their own hostel at London Airport.

630. Reviving the premature ideas of Santos-Dumont and Henri Mignet, French designers produced cheap, easy-to-build, easy-to-fly lightplanes like this Bébé Jodel with a Volkswagen engine. Today, thousands of homebuilt aircraft are flying throughout the world.

631. Gliding, too, has become a highly-popular sport. Costs are much lower than for powered aircraft, and those who fly modern sailplanes come closest to the concept of quiet, graceful bird flight of which the pioneers dreamed.

632. From the start it was clear that aviation would earn big money only when it carried more freight. Operators like the U.S. Flying Tiger Line and British Silver City Airways began specialising in cargo flying in the 'forties. Their loads were made up of flowers, baby chicks, newspapers, fashionable clothes, bullion, perishable food and other items for which speed, elimination of costly packaging and low risk of loss or damage were important. As airliners became bigger, it was possible to make money by packing their freight and baggage holds with cargo when passengers were few. Finally, rates became so low that almost everything began to go by air, and operators had to order all-freight versions of big jets like the Boeing 707 and even the 747 "Jumbo" to cope with the traffic. At airports, special cargo areas had to be built. Today Heathrow handles more passenger and freight in a year than any British sea port except London.

633. B.E.A. pioneered commercial helicopter operation on 21st February 1949 by opening the world's first helicopter night mail service in East Anglia. In June 1950 they began the first scheduled helicopter passenger service between Liverpool and Cardiff. Sikorsky S-51's were used for both.

634. Network of international helicopter passenger services was opened by Sabena in September 1953, linking cities in Belgium, Holland, France and Germany. Small helicopters like this seven-seat Sikorsky S-55 are uneconomical, but large helicopter air buses may one day operate all routes up to 250 miles in length, cutting out time-wasting journeys from city centre to airport.

635. Pioneer approach to flying for all were the cheap-fare flights operated by West African Airways. In 1948–50 all major airlines began Tourist Class services, offering less luxury than First Class flights, but at greatly reduced cost. Still-cheaper 'economy' fares, Family Fare schemes, in which members of a family travelling together pay less, and 'hire-purchase' tickets brought a further boom in air travel.

636. All over the world airports have had t expand rapidly to cope with increased traffi By the early seventies, nearly 500 millio passengers were flying each year on schedule airline services.

The Central Area of London Airpon looked like this in 1957; but already plan were being considered to construct mon passenger handling buildings, to extend th runways, and to switch to a new system i which the aircraft would taxi up to individua finger-shape buildings for loading and un loading. And a second London Airport wa nearing completion at Gatwick in Surrey.

637. New airports and new aircraft wen matched in the mid-1950's by new route Scandinavian Airlines System pioneered completely new era of long-distance flyin when they opened in 1954 the first trans polar route, from Copenhagen to Los Angele via Greenland and Winnipeg. By flying 'Great Circle' course, many hours an saved compared with former routes.

The world really seemed to shrink whe jet-liners like the Boeing 707 (below) bega flying the 'Great Circle' route betwee New York and London in under seven hour

638. Determined to prove its technological progress, Russia planned in 1955 to replace all piston-engined aircraft of its national airline Aeroflot by jet and turboprop types within five years. First hint that Aeroflot would beat the west in offering its passengers regular jet-travel was given when Tupolev Tu-104 twin-jet airliners (right) began to appear in service in 1956. By the following year, Russia had a whole range of new trans-ports in prototype form, including the world's largest airliner, the 120-220 seat, four-turboprop Tu-114.

Key to reduced costs and improved safety may be vertical take-off, which eliminates need for long costly runways and permits slow take-off and landing under radio control in bad weather. First glimpse of the new technique of direct jet lift was given in 1954 by Rolls-Royce's fantastic 'flying bedstead', lifted off the ground by the downward-directed thrust of two jet engines. Future long-range air liners and bombers, and high-speed fighters, may have batteries of small downward-pointing jets to provide vertical take-off and landing. Conventional engines would be used for cruising flight.

Already-existing form of vertical take-off aircraft is the helicopter. Fairey Aviation pointed the way to improved performance and economy in the Roto-dyne by driving the rotor by tip-jets only during take-off and landing. In cruising flight, the Rotodyne was virtually a conventional aeroplane, with half its lift coming from a 'windmilling' rotor and half from fixed wings. Up to 48 passengers could be carried for 230 miles at 185 m.p.h.

641. Rival to the helicopter is the tilt-wing aircraft. First to fly, in 1957, was the Vertol 76, a purely experimental aircraft, with two rotor-propellers driven by a single turboprop engine. For take-off and landing, its wing was tilted vertically as shown, so that it operated as a helicopter. At a safe height, the wing was turned downward, so that the Vertol 76 flew as a normal aeroplane.

642. Pride of the French aircraft industry, the Sud-Aviation Caravelle airliner set a new fashion with its jet-engines mounted on the side of its rear fuselage. Offering reduced cabin noise, easier maintenance and a 'clean' wing, this type of engine installation was adopted for many subsequent types.

643. First to set up a World Speed Record of over 1,000 m.p.h. was the Fairey Delta 2 research aircraft, powered by a Rolls-Royce Avon turbojet. Piloted by Peter Twiss, it achieved an average of 1,132 m.p.h. in two runs on 10th March 1956, beating the previous record by an unprecedented 310 m.p.h. The record stood for 21 months, until a McDonnell Voodoo fighter of the U.S.A.F. attained 1,207 m.p.h. in December 1957.

644. An unprecedented speed for a piloted aeroplane, although not under record conditions, was 2,168 m.p.h. by the Bell X-2 rocket-powered research aircraft in September 1956. It also reached an altitude of 126,200 ft. after being launched at height from the B-50 Superfortress mother-plane under which it is being moved here.

645. The French Trident was a mixed-power interceptor with a rocket motor in its fuselage which was used only for take-off, climb and in combat. A practical endurance was made possible by small wingtip-mounted turbojets. The Trident was armed with a Matra air-to-air guided missile carried under its fuselage.

646–7. For many years the hydrogen bomb has persuaded world leaders to maintain an uneasy policy of peace-through-fear. Now its power is linked with that of the rocket-motor in intercontinental ballistic missiles (ICBM's) against which no defence is yet possible. But, by adapting one of its war rockets as the first stage of the three-stage rocket that launched the *Sputnik I* earth satellite into orbit above our heads on 4th October, 1957, Russia showed that this most complex of man's inventions can be used for peaceful research as well as war.

648. *Sputnik I*, of which a duplicate was exhibited in ~~M~~oscow (*above*), was followed on 3rd November, 1957, by ~~th~~e more ambitious *Sputnik II*, weighing 1,120 lb. and ~~car~~rying a living passenger, the dog Laika. It travelled out ~~nea~~rly 1,000 miles into space before starting to weave its ~~cat~~'s-cradle orbit.

649–50. Many more satellites have followed the two pioneer *Sputniks*. The United States sent the 30 lb. Explorer I into space on 31st January, 1958, and then the first of its Vanguards (*left*) which is expected to remain in orbit for 200 years. The solar batteries built on to its surface power tiny transmitters that have radioed down to Earth vital information on conditions in space. The Vanguard rocket is seen above on the launching pad at Cape Canaveral, Florida.

651. A replica of *Sputnik II* (*right*), seen at the Russian Pavilion at the Brussels Universal and International Exhibition.

652. As the successor to the Bell X-2, American engineers began work on a new rocket-plane known as the X-15 (*left*). It was destined one day to fly at 4,534 m.p.h. The *Sputniks*, too, had set the stage for high adventures to come, although Neil Armstrong could never have imagined that he would set foot on the Moon only twelve years after they were launched. Already, unmanned rockets are heading out beyond Earth orbits, beyond even the Moon and planets, into the boundless emptiness of interplanetary space.

Index to Aircraft

NOTE: *References in italics are to text pages.* *References in roman are to caption numbers.* *References in bold indicate illustrations.*

Index to Personalities

Acknowledgments

This history could not have been compiled without the full and generous co-operation of aircraft manufacturers, airlines and air forces all over the world. To them, and to the many other friends who have offered pictures from their treasured collections of personal photographs, we offer our sincere thanks. Our only regret is that we could use so few of them.

The source of most of the illustrations is given in the following list. Others are from the author's own collection.

Admiralty, 616, 617
Aeronautics, 32, 71
The Aeroplane, 416, 418, 476, 540
Air France, 301, 343, 344, 384
The Air Ministry, 243, 326, 341, 397, 398, 425, 619, 620, 621, 624
Associated Newspapers Ltd., 111
Associated Press, 361, 512, 531, 647
B.E.A., 577, 578, 587, 636
Bell Aircraft Corporation, 561, 568, 644
Air Vice-Marshal D. C. T. Bennett, 400, 462, 528
Blackburn and General Aircraft Ltd., 93, 394
B.O.A.C., 435, 461, 484, 584, 588
Boeing Airplane Company, 299, 334, 388, 390, 402, 433, 437, 439, 457, 553, 566, 571, 583, 607, 637
Lord Brabazon of Tara, 72, 73, 106
The Bristol Aeroplane Co., Ltd., 116, 117, 122, 150, 153, 193, 194, 226, 284, 285, 403, 451, 635
The late Air Chief Marshal Sir Robert Brooke-Popham, 161, 164, 219, 281, 283
Charles E. Brown, 396, 448, 449, 450, 520, 525, 526, 527
Canadian Department of Defence (R.C.A.F.), 125, 195, 483
Central Press Photos, 104, 109, 110, 563
Chance Vought Aircraft, 395
Convair, 569, 606, 608, 611, 613, 614, 646
The de Havilland Aircraft Co., Ltd., 119, 354, 374, 375, 376, 436, 513
The de Havilland Aircraft of Canada Ltd., 604
Douglas Aircraft Company Inc., 332, 333, 350, 351, 456, 463, 565
The English Electric Co., Ltd., 626
Col. P. T. Etherton, 405
The Fairey Aviation Co., Ltd., 340, 369, 455, 640, 643
Flight, 66, 91, 92, 105, 134, 159, 168, 191, 192, 200, 205, 218, 271, 327, 357, 370, 371, 373, 414, 430, 453, 454, 475, 486, 489, 631, 638
The Flying Tiger Line, 632
Fokker, 129
Fox Photos, 487
The General Electric Co., Ltd., 148
Mr. C. H. Gibbs-Smith, 39
Gloster Aircraft Co., Ltd., 347, 559
Mr. E. C. Gordon-England, 188
The G. Q. Parachute Co., Ltd., 231, 232
Mr. William Green, 444, 464, 550, 555, 560, 562
Handley Page Ltd., 94, 297, 298, 337
Hawker Aircraft Ltd., 167, 223, 235, 252, 264, 523
Mr. Hugo Hooftmann, 362
Hunting Percival Aircraft Ltd., 474
The Imperial War Museum, 213, 224, 225, 227, 234, 236, 240, 241, 244, 245, 246, 248, 249, 251, 253, 254, 255, 257, 258, 259, 260, 261, 262, 263, 266, 267, 268, 269, 270, 273, 276, 278, 279, 280, 282, 287, 490, 494, 495, 496, 497, 498, 501, 503, 507, 508, 509, 510, 514, 515, 516, 518, 521, 522, 524, 532, 533, 534, 535, 538, 543, 544, 545, 546, 547, 548, 549, 551, 552, 554
The Italian Air Attaché in London, General C. F. de Porto, 423, 426, 556, 557
Kaman Aircraft Corporation, 409, 410
K.L.M. Royal Dutch Airlines, 304, 434
The Lockheed Aircraft Corporation, 335, 392, 419, 420, 477, 530, 564, 570, 582, 610
The Martin Company, 324, 325, 438, 537, 615
The Maxim Silencer Company, 19, 20
Ministry of Supply, 37
D. Napier and Son, 623
National Geographic Society (U.S.A.), 468
Monsieur Jacques Noetinger, 422, 479, 504, 505, 630, 642, 645
North American Aviation Inc., 567, 602, 610, 652
Mr. Cyril Peckham, 372
Pest Control Ltd., 628
Major Henry Petre, 173, 237
Pictorial Press, 452
Picture Post Library, 1, 3, 4, 5, 6, 7, 8, 9, 10, 11, 12, 16, 18, 23, 31, 33, 34, 35, 36, 38, 40, 41, 42, 43, 44, 45, 46, 47, 48, 49, 50, 51, 52, 53, 54, 55, 57, 59, 60, 62, 67, 68, 69, 70, 74, 81, 83, 85, 86, 87, 88, 89, 95, 96, 98, 99, 100, 101, 102, 103, 107, 108, 112, 113, 114, 115, 118, 120, 121, 123, 124, 127, 131, 132, 133, 140, 141, 142, 143, 144, 145, 146, 147, 149, 152, 157, 162, 163, 171, 172, 174, 175, 176, 177, 178, 179, 180, 181, 182, 183, 184, 185, 187, 189, 198, 201, 202, 203, 204, 206, 207, 209, 210, 211, 212, 256, 274, 275, 295, 296, 302, 303, 328, 329, 330, 338, 342, 358, 359, 360, 363, 365, 366, 404, 411, 428, 446, 447, 558, 589, 590, 591
Republic Aviation Corporation, 605, 627
A. V. Roe and Co., Ltd., 79, 160, 166, 222, 593, 625
Rolls-Royce Ltd., 272, 292, 586, 639
Royal Aeronautical Society, 13, 130, 427
Sabena, 320, 321, 355, 356, 634
Saunders-Roe Ltd., 190
The Science Museum, 14, 15, 17, 22
Mr. H. (Jerry) Shaw, 319
Shell, 622
Short Brothers and Harland Ltd., 76, 90, 151, 154, 155, 156, 336, 406, 458, 460
Mr. Oswald Short, 75, 158
Mr. Igor Sikorsky, 58, 214, 215, 216, 217, 481
Silver City Airways Ltd., 580
The Smithsonian Institution, 24, 25, 26, 27, 28, 29, 64, 65
The Sperry Gyroscope Company Ltd., 196, 197, 239
Sport and General Press Agency Ltd., 349
Mr. Whitney Straight, 485
Swissair, 126, 318, 352
Mrs. J. T. Taylor, 221
Topical Press Photos, 289, 393
Mr. Geoffrey Tyson, 471, 472
United Air Lines, 300, 385, 386, 387, 389, 391
United States Department of Defence and Information Services, 30, 135, 136, 137, 138, 139, 186, 290, 353, 368, 465, 529, 542, 592, 594, 595, 597, 598, 599, 600, 601, 612, 618, 649, 650
Vertol Aircraft Corporation, 641
Sir Alliott Verdon Roe, 77, 78
Vickers-Armstrongs Ltd., 165, 229, 293, 294, 412, 478, 493, 517
Monsieur Vreedenburgh, 128
Mr. J. Y. Watson, 169, 170
Westland Aircraft Ltd., 585
Major G. E. Woods Humphery, 306, 307, 308, 309, 310, 311, 312, 313, 345, 346, 377, 378, 379, 380, 381, 382, 383